*Twayne's English Authors Series*

Sylvia E. Bowman, *Editor*

INDIANA UNIVERSITY

*Israel Zangwill*

ISRAEL ZANGWILL

# Israel Zangwill

By ELSIE BONITA ADAMS

*Wisconsin State University-Whitewater*

Twayne Publishers, Inc.    ::    New York

To Professor Calvin G. Thayer

# Preface

In the fall of 1962, while I was commuting daily in and out of Boston on the Metropolitan Transit Authority, I hit on a plan to pass the tedious travel hours—namely, reading minor British novels of the late nineteenth century. Being somewhat compulsive, I decided to give coherence to the project by reading every novel mentioned in the chapter on "The Novel: Naturalism and Romance" in A. C. Baugh's *Literary History of England.* And, while I was patiently working my way through such books as William Hale White's *Autobiography of Mark Rutherford,* Mrs. Humphrey Ward's *Robert Elsmere,* Joseph Henry Shorthouse's *John Inglesant,* and Richard Whiteing's *No. 5 John Street,* I discovered Israel Zangwill.

*Children of the Ghetto* hit me with the force with which it must have struck readers of the 1890's, who were on the same literary diet I had been following. In the company of other minor writers of the late nineteenth century, Zangwill stood out: his work still had emotive power and relevance to life. Yet who was reading him anymore? Somewhat to my disappointment, I soon learned that other scholars knew of Zangwill and that he was still read by more people than I would have initially supposed. However, I also learned that no one had for over forty years undertaken a critical analysis of his work. My recreational reading suddenly became a scholarly pursuit.

Fortunately, during the past ten or so years, there has been a kind of minor renaissance in Zangwill scholarship. AMS Press, Inc., has reprinted Zangwill's *Collected Works* in a fourteen-volume set. A book-length biography of Zangwill by Joseph Leftwich was published in 1957; a selected bibliography of Zangwill's work was compiled by Annamarie Peterson and published in *The Bulletin of Bibliography and Magazine Notes* in 1961; and in 1964 appeared Maurice Wohlgelernter's *Israel Zangwill: A Study,* which contains some literary criticism but chiefly focuses on Zang-will's ideas. I am heavily indebted to these scholars for factual in-formation about Zangwill's life and works. For information about Zangwill's ideas, however, I rely on Zangwill himself; and the literary criticism in the following study is my own.

My principal aim in this book is to explicate as objectively and completely as possible the literary works of Zangwill. Because Zangwill's canon provides numerous examples of every literary genre, I have arranged the chapters—except for the introduction and conclusion—according to types of literature. In my comments I have tried to avoid overestimating Zangwill's literary accom-plishments, for much of Zangwill has been deservedly forgotten. On the other hand, I make a case for the reinstatement of his best works to a prominent place in late Victorian and Edwardian studies. Certainly, *Children of the Ghetto* and selected short stories from *"They That Walk in Darkness"* and *Ghetto Comedies* ought to be revived. The reader interested in modern Jewish writers such as Saul Bellow, Philip Roth, or Bernard Malamud will find much in Zangwill to admire.

ELSIE BONITA ADAMS

*Whitewater, Wisconsin*

# Acknowledgments

I wish to express my gratitude to all those who helped make this book possible. I am most indebted to my husband, George, for his advice, assistance, encouragement, patience, and good humor. Especial thanks go to Professors Calvin G. Thayer, A. J. Fritz, J. L. Kendall, and others who made my years of study at the University of Oklahoma particularly rewarding. I am also grateful to Professor Saul Levin, of the State University of New York at Binghamton, for teaching me to read Hebrew; to Mr. Morris Gitlitz, Binghamton, New York, for his translation of Yiddish criticism of Zangwill; to Professor Sylvia E. Bowman, for her helpful commentary on my manuscript; to Mrs. Donna Lewis, who typed the manuscript several times over; to the libraries at the State University of New York at Binghamton, Cornell University, and the University of Wisconsin, whose facilities enabled me to complete my research on Zangwill; and to Wisconsin State University—Whitewater, for reducing my teaching load from twelve to nine hours while I was writing the book.

For permission to quote from the works of Israel Zangwill, I make grateful acknowledgment to the executors of the Zangwill Estate: Professor O. L. Zangwill, University of Cambridge; Miss J. Hope-Wallace, London; and Mr. A. I. Zangwill, Plainfield, New Jersey. I also gratefully acknowledge the following for permission to quote from copyrighted material:

Columbia University Press: from Maurice Wohlgelernter, *Israel Zangwill: A Study;*

Dover Publications, Inc.: from Rabbi Maurice Wohlgelernter's Introduction to *The King of Schnorrers* by Israel Zangwill, Dover Publications, Inc., New York, 1965. Reprinted through permission of the publisher.

Harcourt Brace Jovanovich, Inc.: from Edward Wallant, *The Human Season;*

The Jewish Publication Society of America: from *Selected Religious Poems of Solomon ibn Gabirol,* translated by Israel Zangwill and edited by Israel Davidson, 1944;
The Society of Authors, as agent for the Bernard Shaw Estate: from Bernard Shaw, *Major Barbara.*

# Contents

# Chronology

1864    Israel Zangwill born on January 21 in Whitechapel ghetto, London, of immigrant parents—his father, Moses Zangwill, from Latvia; his mother, Ellen Hannah Marks, from Poland. Received his early schooling in Bristol, where family moved soon after Zangwill's birth.

1872–  Family returned to London. Zangwill attended Jews' Free
1888    School in Whitechapel, where he eventually became a pupil-teacher.

1882    Won prize money from a publication called *Society* for a humorous story, "Professor Grimmer," published serially. Published in collaboration with Louis Cowen a pamphlet, *Motza Kleis,* describing East End market days; also published anonymously a comic ballad, *The Ballad of Moses.*

c. 1883–  Edited and wrote for an annual, *Purim.*
1885

1884    Received a degree from London University, with honors in French, English, and Mental and Moral Science.

1888    Resigned his teaching position at the Jews' Free School. Began column, "Morour and Charousoth," for *The Jewish Standard* (continued until 1891). *The Premier and the Painter,* in collaboration with Louis Cowen, published under the pseudonym "J. Freeman Bell." Two short stories, "Under Sentence of Marriage" and "Satan Mekatrig," published pseudonymously.

1889    Wrote "English Judaism" for *Jewish Quarterly Review,* an essay instrumental in getting him a commission to write *Children of the Ghetto.*

1890–  Edited *Ariel,* a humorous paper.
1892

1891    *The Bachelors' Club* published; Zangwill's first recognized success. *The Big Bow Mystery* published serially in the *London Star.*

1892   *The Old Maids' Club; Children of the Ghetto.* Two play-
lets, *The Great Demonstration* (in collaboration with Louis
Cowen) and *Six Persons,* produced in London. Contributed (for several years) to Jerome K. Jerome's humor
magazine, *The Idler.*

1893   *Ghetto Tragedies, The King of Schnorrers* (serially in *The
Idler*), and *Merely Mary Ann* (*A Tale*). Began monthly
column, "Without Prejudice," for *Pall Mall Magazine*
(continued to 1896).

1894   *The King of Schnorrers: Grotesques and Fantasies* published. Began column, "Men, Women and Books," for
*The Critic* (New York, continued to 1896).

1895   Met Theodore Herzl and joined the Zionist movement.
*The Master* (which had appeared serially in *Harper's
Weekly,* 1894) published.

1896   *Without Prejudice.*

1898   *Dreamers of the Ghetto; The Celibates' Club.* Traveled in
the United States as lecturer.

1899   Dramatized *Children of the Ghetto,* produced in New York
and London. *"They That Walk in Darkness": Ghetto
Tragedies.*

1900   *The Mantle of Elijah;* one-act tragedy, *The Moment of
Death* (also called *The Moment Before*) produced in New
York.

1901   A three-act comedy, *The Revolted Daughter,* produced in
London.

1903   Married on November 26 Edith Ayrton, herself an author.
*The Grey Wig: Stories and Novelettes* and *Blind Children*
published. Supported the "Uganda Plan" at Sixth Zionist
Congress at Basel.

1904   Dramatic version of *The Serio-Comic Governess* published;
produced in New York. *Merely Mary Ann* (*A Play*) also
published and produced.

1905   A drama, *Jinny the Carrier,* produced in Boston. Founded
the Jewish Territorial Organization (ITO) after Seventh
Zionist Congress rejected the "Uganda Plan."

1906   *Nurse Marjorie* produced in New York.

1907   *Ghetto Comedies.* Continued work with Jewish Territorial
Organization.

1908   *The Melting Pot* produced in Washington, D. C.

1909   Traveled in Italy. *The Melting Pot;* produced in New York.
1910   *Italian Fantasies.*
1911   *The War God;* produced in London.
1912   *The Next Religion;* produced in London, banned by the censor.
1914   London premier of *The Melting Pot. Plaster Saints* produced in London and published.
1916   *The War for the World.*
1917   *The Principle of Nationalities* (Conway Memorial Lecture).
1918   Delivered the Arthur Davis Memorial Lecture for Jewish Historical Society of England (published as *Chosen Peoples*). *Too Much Money* produced in London (published 1924).
1919   The novel *Jinny the Carrier.*
1920   *The Voice of Jerusalem.*
1921   *The Cockpit.*
1922   *The Forcing House; or The Cockpit Continued.*
1923   Visited New York, delivered the *Watchman, What of the Night?* address to American Jewish Congress. Translations of *Selected Religious Poems of Solomon ibn Gabirol* published. *The Forcing House* produced in London. Began a novel, *The Baron of Offenbach* (never finished).
1924   *We Moderns* produced in New York. Returned to England for venture in theater management.
1925   ITO dissolved. *We Moderns;* produced in London.
1926   Failures and frustrations of theater management contributed to a nervous breakdown. Died August 1 at Midhurst, Sussex.

# CHAPTER 1

# *A Ghetto Englishman*

❝What he will be in another ten years, if he continues to develop at the rate of the last three, passes comprehension,❞ a critic wrote of Israel Zangwill in 1894.[1] The enthusiasm of the critic's statement is indicative of the accolades the young essayist, novelist, and short-story writer was receiving throughout the 1890's in England. In 1894, Zangwill's fame rested on a highly successful collection of stories published in Henry and Company's Library of Wit and Humour, a realistic novel of life in the London ghetto which was "the most talked of book of the season,"[2] and short stories published as *Ghetto Tragedies*, which were hailed by the influential American critic and novelist, William Dean Howells, as "among the very finest work produced in our time."[3] Even critics skeptical of Zangwill's artistry were admitting that he had talent and promise.

And the praise continued; he was hailed as "The Dickens of the ghetto," "the foremost writer of the day in England," "one of the foremost among the band of modern writers," a man with "the large interest in life detached from himself which has been the inspiration of all great, as distinguished from little, masters of fiction," the "most striking" Anglo-Jewish genius since Disraeli, "in the front rank of English novelists," "of that aristocracy to which the greatest of writers belong," "one of the mightiest intellects of modern times."[4] In a book entitled *Victorian Novelists*, published at the end of the century, James Oliphant, who thought that Thomas Hardy would never be considered a great artist, devoted a chapter to Rudyard Kipling and Israel Zangwill because their "quality of work gives promise of high achievement."[5] Zangwill's fame at the turn of the century was not limited to England; in 1898 he visited the United States on a lecture tour and, according to the American writer Hamlin Garland, "It made the Spanish war a stale drama for the time."[6] Reminiscing years later about this visit, Garland reiterated: "No recent visitor had so deeply stirred our literary circles." Notably, Garland includes Zangwill in his list of "the outstanding English writers" at the end of the century, along with Thomas Hardy, Henry James, James Barrie, Bernard Shaw, and Rudyard Kipling.[7]

The fact that Zangwill today is little known in literary circles would have in an earlier age inspired an essay on fame, probably spoken by Philosophia. Instead, in a more prosaic age, we note that his reputation declined gradually during the opening decades of the century, and it declined significantly after his death in 1926. The obituaries of Zangwill indicate that at his death his literary reputation was still alive,[8] though one observation in the New York *Bookman* tells us that by 1926 it was rapidly dying: "He had a great vogue when I was a little boy," the columnist wrote.[9] It is as though with Zangwill's death the world agreed to forget a man who only a quarter century earlier had been ranked with Shaw, Hardy, and Kipling. His books went out of print; for years no literary critics wrote about him; and, though American historians remembered his characterization of America as "the melting pot" and though Jews remembered his place in the Zionist movement, Zangwill became a very minor figure in histories of literature. For example, he receives in *A Literary History of England* one sentence in the chapter "The Novel: Naturalism and Romance."[10]

The rise and decline of Zangwill's literary reputation suggest two questions which have to be answered in the following chapters. First, what was there in his work that created the immense enthusiasm for him in the 1890's? And second, was the decline in reputation warranted? *Why* his reputation declined is a related question, but that can be answered at the outset. In order to do so, some brief commentary about his life and work is helpful.

## I  *Realist and Humorist*

Zangwill was born of immigrant parents in the Whitechapel ghetto of London. Though he spent part of his childhood in Bristol, where his parents moved shortly after his birth, he returned to the London ghetto with his family and spent his adolescence studying at the Jews' Free School in Whitechapel, eventually becoming a pupil-teacher there. Life in the London ghetto at the end of the nineteenth century was one of transition; for the newcomers from eastern Europe were trying to preserve the tradition and culture of the ghettos they had come from against new economic and cultural conditions forcing change. Favorable to change were the English Jews who had been assimilated into English life and the younger generation—the children of the ghetto—educated in public schools.[11] From his experience of this ghetto in transition, Zangwill derived the richest materials for his art; in the conflict between tradition and change, between the old generation and the new, he found themes which form the basis of his best fiction. In Judaism, with its emphasis on family and social responsibility and with its faith in the unity of God, he found values which governed all his work. Because he was himself a child of the ghetto—born there, educated there—he was able in *Children of the Ghetto, The King of Schnorrers, Ghetto Tragedies, Ghetto Comedies,* and *Dreamers of the Ghetto* to re-create for a fascinated world the character and life of the ghetto.

Zangwill's earliest recognition, however, was not for his ghetto fiction but for his work in what was then called the "New Humor." Zangwill was part of an era which had a passion for the adjective "New"; there was the "New Hedonism," a "New Journalism," the "New Woman," *art nouveau,* the "New Imperialism," and there was also the "New Humor." Zangwill's first novel was a humorous work, *The Premier and the Painter,* written in collaboration with a friend and fellow teacher at the Jews' Free School and published in 1888; the novel was a comic-satiric attack on politics, the press, and a plethora of human follies; and it had the puns, inverted epigrams, exaggeration, and lavish detail that characterized Zangwill's prose long after the New Humor had disappeared. In the early 1890's, Zangwill edited a humor magazine, *Ariel,* and wrote regularly for *The Idler,* another humor magazine, in which he published essays, stories, and his comic masterpiece, *The King of Schnorrers.*

The publication in 1891 of a collection of stories called *The Bachelors' Club,* which had originally appeared in *Ariel,* established Zangwill's reputation as a wit and raconteur. His technique is described in a review of *The Celibates' Club* in 1898: "the journalistic talent for writing up exhaustively from the slightest foundation of facts or fancy."[12] Though Zangwill never lost all traces of the style that he cultivated in his works associated with the New Humor, he did, fortunately, abandon the trivial and facetious for serious humor: comedy with a point. His ghetto fiction contains humor better classified as "Jewish" than as "New." This humor is, as Bernard Schilling observes, born from suffering—comic relief from the "monstrous unspeakable joke" played on the Jews through centuries of frustrated action and cruel persecution.[13] Thus Zangwill's ghetto "comedies" are bittersweet, and his best attempts at humor are often edged with satire.

Zangwill's ghetto fiction—indeed, all his fiction—lacks the pervasive pessimism characteristic of other end-of-the-century Realistic fiction. This is partly because Zangwill regarded humor as an essential part of life, without which one misrepresented reality, and partly because Zangwill's world view affirmed the values of love, home, and faith. Life is not, Zangwill insisted, all unmitigated pain, nor is it filled with unrelieved tragedy; it has also elements of comedy—both absurdity and joy; in the ghetto he found "tragedies of spiritual struggle, comedies of material ambition."[14] In his work, he tried to capture the sense of life's complexity by showing its sordidness, its beauty, its pain, its joy, its failure, its successes, its everyday reality, and its dreams. In classifying Zangwill as a Realist, therefore, one must add that he was also humorist, anatomist, Romanticist—all of which are, according to Zangwill, characteristic of one who honestly looks at reality.

## II  *Social Critic and Zionist*

In defining Zangwill's place in his era, Holbrook Jackson's history of the 1890's is useful. Jackson outlines three characteristics of the decade: "the so-called Decadence; the introduction of a Sense of Fact into literature and art; and the development of a Transcendental View of Social Life."[15] Zangwill's choice and treatment of subjects align him with the second, and his faith in society's capacity for reform align him with the third. Zangwill rejected any attitude, like the decadent's, which urged withdrawal or retreat from social responsibilities or which found value—esthetic pleasure—in decay and collapse. And precisely this feeling that every man ought to actively participate in the life of his time led to Zangwill's eclipse as an artist. For, at the turn of the century, Zangwill stopped writing short stories and novels to devote his attention to politics and social reform. In the twentieth century, Zangwill dedicated his talent almost exclusively to speaking about controversial issues, to writing persuasive and analytical essays on sometimes unpopular topics, and to producing plays heavily laden —sometimes burdened—with social commentary.

Maurice Wohlgelernter in *Israel Zangwill: A Study* attributes Zangwill's change from artist to social critic to two factors: his meeting of Theodore Herzl in 1895 and his marriage to Edith Ayrton in 1903.[16] The meeting with Herzl changed the direction of Zangwill's commitment to the Jews: before this occasion, Zangwill had familiarized the English world with Jewish life through his fiction; after it, he began active work in the international Zionist movement. And his "mixed marriage" to Edith Ayrton, herself a novelist and active in the Feminist movement, led to Zangwill's increasing concern for a world religion of brotherhood and love, in which Christians and Jews, men and women, have equal rights. His Zionist work and World War I turned Zangwill's attention to international politics, and his opinions about the necessity for disarmament, the horror of war, the failure of diplomacy, and the imperative need for tolerance of minority opinion alienated many former admirers. And, finally, his break with Zionism caused him to fall into disfavor with many Jews.

With Herzl, Zangwill was one of the early leaders of the Zionist movement, which had as its goal the securing of a Jewish state. But in 1903 Zangwill became the center of a controversy over where the Jewish state was to be located, a controversy which divided the Zionist movement. At the time, Palestine was in the hands of the Turkish government; and the possibility of Jewish autonomy in Palestine seemed out of the question. But pogroms in Russia had made the need for a Jewish homeland immediate and imperative. Therefore, when England's colonial secretary, Joseph Chamberlain, offered Herzl part of Kenya for Jewish settlement, Herzl, Zangwill, and other leaders presented the plan (called the "Uganda Plan") to the Sixth Zionist Congress at Basel (1903).

The result was a fierce debate between the supporters of the Uganda Plan and the Zionists who argued that "It is not Palestine, and it will never be Palestine."[17] The Sixth Congress voted to send a commission to Uganda to investigate, but at the Seventh Congress in 1905, the Uganda Plan was rejected. Zangwill then broke from the Zionists to devote himself to the Jewish Territorial Organization (the ITO), which had as its primary object the obtaining of an autonomous Jewish homeland anywhere in the world. Directing this organization, Zangwill argued that Palestine was not essential to Zionism; for "Zion is where the Jew lives as a Jew."[18] At the same time that he was searching for a homeland for displaced Jews, Zangwill was pleading for the toleration and acceptance of the Jews of the Diaspora. His famous play, *The Melting Pot* (1909), expressed his hope that America could provide a place where the Judeo-Christian ideal of the brotherhood of all men could be realized. The play was, however, a kind of wish-fulfillment fantasy for Zangwill, who became progressively disillusioned about the possibility of a society—in America or in Europe—in which love and reason would rule. World War I convinced him that Christianity had failed to realize its master's ideals of love and peace; and Zangwill, like many of his fictional protagonists, turned once more to the ideals of Judaism as the sole source of his faith in world unity.

In Wohlgelernter's recent book and in other critical appraisals of Zangwill, much stress is placed on his inconsistency of thought and on his ability to reconcile apparently contradictory beliefs. It is true that he was both Zionist and patriotic Englishman, a skeptic with a deeply religious view, a contemplative and active man—a man not at ease in a world of disintegrating values. Wohlgelernter feels that Zangwill's contradictions arise from his "Jewish mind placed in a nineteenth-century setting."[19] But that, in my opinion, places too much emphasis on Zangwill's uniqueness. He was not only a child of the ghetto but also a child of the nineteenth century. He reflects the conflict between skepticism and belief, between esthetic and active pursuits, between a Realistic and Romantic view of life common to most Victorian writers.

Holbrook Jackson correctly places him among those late nineteenth-century artists who "sprang into existence out of the *Zeitgeist.*"[20] And, when the spirit of the 1890's died, so did Zangwill the artist. Today Zangwill appears in studies of Jewish literature and in histories of the Zionist movement, but he is a footnote in English literary history. After his death, it was thirty-one years before a biography of him appeared; and it was thirty-eight years before a book-length critical study of him appeared, one described by a reviewer as "the first (and quite possibly, I suppose, the last) full-length critical study of Zangwill's work."[21] The following pages demonstrate that it was not the last and, hopefully, that it ought not to have been.

## CHAPTER 2

# Fantasies, Criticism, and Philosophical Excursions

M any contemporary critics of Zangwill see his importance as historical, not literary; these critics therefore most value Zangwill's essays, especially his social criticism. Today Zangwill is certainly better known among historians of ideas than among literary critics, and the predominant feeling is that "the only satisfactory study of Zangwill . . . is one which . . . concentrates on his personality and historical significance."[1]

Like numerous other end-of-the-century Realists, Zangwill divided his time between journalism and fiction. In the 1880's and early 1890's, he wrote for limited circulation periodicals: under the pseudonym "Baroness von S.," he contributed items for an annual, *Myer's Calendar and Diary* (also called *The Jewish Calendar*); under the pseudonym "Marshallik," he prepared a column for *The Jewish Standard;* he also edited and wrote for *Ariel,* a humorous weekly. In 1889 Zangwill contributed an essay on "English Judaism" to the first volume of the *Jewish Quarterly Review,* an essay which Lucien Wolf says convinced the newly founded Jewish Publication Society of Philadelphia that Zangwill was the man to write a novel about modern Jewish life and which consequently led to Zangwill's commission to write *Children of the Ghetto.*[2]

After the appearance of *Children of the Ghetto* in 1892, Zangwill's fame was assured. In the 1890's he wrote for numerous popular magazines—contributing items to the New Humor magazine *The Idler;* writing a column "Men, Women and Books" for *The Critic* (New York); and preparing a regular monthly column, "Without Prejudice," for *The Pall Mall Magazine.* The young writer who, according to his own account, began journalism in the 1880's "at the very bottom and entirely unassisted"[3] had by the middle of the 1890's become one of the most popular columnists in the London literary world. In "My First Book," written for *The Idler,* Zangwill brags that, since 1891, he has "never written a line anywhere that has not been purchased before it was written."[4]

Zangwill wrote on almost every controversial subject of his day: he attacked corruption in modern politics, the misuse of wealth, the failure of international diplomacy, and the nationalistic aspirations which lead to war; he championed women's rights and the brotherhood of man; he spent much of his lifetime protesting the mistreatment of his people and urging a homeland for the Jews. His artistic range as essayist was not limited, however, to social criticism; his journalistic writing also includes essays of playful whimsy, literary causeries, fantasies, rhapsodies, and satiric-ironic fables for our time. Many of his essays are uncollected, but his principal methods and ideas are illustrated in perhaps too copious detail in *Without Prejudice* (1896), a selection of Zangwill's contributions to *The Pall Mall Magazine; Italian Fantasies* (1910), a collection of miscellaneous essays that grew out of his 1909 trip to Italy; *The War for the World* (1916), a collection of essays and poems dealing with world politics, the disaster of World War I, women's rights, and the Jewish problem; *The Principle of Nationalities* (1917), a Conway Memorial Lecture in which Zangwill maintains that nationalism is wrecking Europe; *Chosen Peoples* (1918), a lecture for the Jewish Historical Society in which he defines the mission of Judaism as "world-service"; and *The Voice of Jerusalem* (1920), essays dealing with the nature of Jewish idealism, the necessity for a Jewish homeland, and the failure of the world to achieve a sense of community, of brotherhood.

## I  *Essays for* The Idler, The Critic, *and* The Pall Mall Magazine

In his earliest journalistic work Zangwill was associated with the New Humor of Jerome K. Jerome, Robert Barr, Barry Pain, and others who have disappeared from even the footnotes of literary history. Beginning in February, 1892, Zangwill wrote for *The Idler,* edited by Jerome and Barr. A perusal of the pages of this magazine reveals that the humor was not new, nor was it even always amusing. Zangwill's contributions include several short stories which were later included in collections, most of them in *The King of Schnorrers: Grotesques and Fantasies.* In Volume IV (1893–94) of *The Idler, The King of Schnorrers* appears in monthly installments; and Zangwill items appear regularly in a column called "The Idlers' Club." Illustrative of his efforts for "The Idlers' Club" are a criticism of Oscar Wilde couched in Wildean epigrams and reversals ("You are much too important to be discussed seriously"); the ironic defense of "Somewhere Else" as "the ideal resort"; or a parody of a Renaissance defense of tobacco in "Zangwill reasoneth with ye monarch." For the most part, Zangwill's essays in *The Idler*, though sometimes clever, are seldom distinguished in content or style.

His column, "Men, Women and Books," for *The Critic* (September, 1894–December, 1896) is of interest because of its sound, often witty, and very readable literary criticism. An example of Zangwill's technique as literary critic is his review of *Marcella,* a three-volume novel by the popular writer, Mrs. Humphrey Ward. Zangwill shows in this review an appreciation for Mrs. Ward's "talent and industry" in anatomizing a segment of English life, but he perceives her major weaknesses: tedium and pseudointellectualism. He describes precisely the feelings one has in reading Mrs. Humphrey Ward: "One rises from a novel of hers distinctly older. In the middle of the second volume one wonders vaguely how many aeons ago one was reading the first, and what infinities are to traverse before one will emerge from the third."[5] Other reviews in "Men, Women and Books" are equally incisive in their critical judgments and imaginative in expression.

The essays in *The Critic* are also of interest because they, along with those which Zangwill was writing at the same time in "Without Prejudice," contain his theory of art, a theory which places his own fiction, drama, and poetry outside the *fin-de-siècle* school of "art for art's sake" and within the stream of art for life's sake. To Zangwill, art was realistic (though not without elements of romance), serious (though necessarily touched by humor), and large. In a review of Turgenev's *Daughter of Joy* he comments on the nature of art: to him, "merely artistic" renderings of incident are not great art; for "A work of art that has no general relation to reality is only a toy, a luxury, and the maker thereof is veritably a 'Daughter of Joy.' "[6]

Reality, however, to Zangwill consists of more than the external world of the senses; life is, he says in an essay in *Without Prejudice,* "large, chaotic, inexpressible, not to be bound down by a formula."[7] Expressing in criticism a theory that he gave full expression in his novel *The Master,* Zangwill insists always on the artist's need to grasp the mystery, the romance, of everyday reality. Thus he admires Robert Louis Stevenson's depiction in *The Ebb-Tide* of "the romance of the modern"[8] or Maurice Maeterlinck's portrayal in *L'Interieur* of "the mystery that lies at the root of the simplest human life."[9] Though Zangwill admires the purity and perfection of the prose style of Walter Pater, he finds Pater lacking in breadth; according to Zangwill, Pater allows "only a select fraction of the cosmos to have the entry to his consciousness," and he "mistakes University for Universe."[10] To Zangwill, art is a combination of the mysterious and the mundane; at its best, it captures both the beauty and the ugliness, the seriousness and the humor, of life.

Zangwill's art theory also appears in essays collected in *Without Prejudice.* As in "Men, Women and Books," Zangwill paints a picture of the artist as a somewhat prosaic man who sees truly, works hard, lives an active life, and accepts money for his work. "Art in England" urges a combination of the man of action and the man of letters; "Bohemia and Verlaine" stresses the homely, hard-working nature of an artist, on whom nothing in life should be lost; "The Philosophy of Topsy-Turveydom" attacks Oscar Wilde for attitudinizing (and makes what may be the most tasteless accidental pun in all literature when Zangwill says, "What you want is a little knowledge of life, and twelve months' hard labour"); "Authors and Publishers" defends the artist's right to monetary reward for his labor.

In *Without Prejudice,* Zangwill also begins what was to be a lifelong onslaught against shortsighted politics. In "Concerning General Elections," he attacks the party system and suggests as an improvement a non-elected body to propose measures and the people—not their representatives—to vote on them; he argues that universal suffrage has brought not democracy but only a purging of mass discontent. "The Abolition of Money" depicts a utopia in which all men are workers and traders, having discovered that they could live on little "and that it was better for all to get it than for some to continue to want it" (126). "Budapest" defines true nationalism as a country's ability to absorb and make patriots of her foreigners, an idea which was to receive expansion in Zangwill's political dramas as well as in countless speeches and essays.

In addition to the essays on art and politics, *Without Prejudice* contains a variety of essay forms, including a dream vision ("A Vision of the Burden of Man"), a reminiscence of past joys ("Tuning Up"), a semiserious "Defense of Gambling," a long monologue ("Opinions of the Young Fogey"), a facetious system for choosing dinner partners ("Table-Talk"), and a catalogue of "Societies to Found." Finally, in assessing the artistic value of *Without Prejudice,* one can agree with the anonymous critic for *The Bookman* (New York) who found the book "encyclopaedic," witty, versatile, stimulating, but lacking "that last gift of the genius and the artist, the gift of omission."[11]

## II  Italian Fantasies

*Italian Fantasies,* which is no less generous in its offerings, includes "A Rhapsody by Way of Prelude," "fantasies" ("Fantasia Napolitana: Being a Reverie of Aquariums, Museums, and Dead Christs"), "excursions" ("Into the Grotesque: With a Glance at Maps and Modern Fallacies" and "Into Heaven and Hell: With a Depreciation of Dante"), and subjects touching almost every facet of Zangwill's philosophy. Many of the essays invite an analogy between the prose fantasies and musical form: the opening essay is "A Rhapsody"; the second, a "Fantasia"; the third, "A Capriccio"; later essays are entitled "Intermezzo" and "Variations on a Theme." With few exceptions, the essays with musical titles exemplify Zangwill at his worst: they are associative in organization, informal in tone, whimsical in content, and, as one critic complained, "shockingly overwritten."[12] The style is indeed "rhapsodic," utilizing repetition, exclamations, many questions, interruptions, involuted sentences, and archaisms; the humor is often labored and lame.

Fortunately, most of the essays in the collection are serious explorations of artistic, social, and religious problems, and in these Zangwill is at his best. For example, the third essay, "The Carpenter's Wife: A Capriccio," avoids the "neo-Carlylese" of the opening essays and pointedly comments on the failure of institutionalized religion. The writer, on his way from Vicenza to the Church of Our Lady of the Mountain, meets in a vision a Jewish maiden who takes him to a Jewish home in Galilee; he witnesses a *Seder* meal in the home of Yussef and Miriam, Christ's parents, who are appalled at their eldest's heresies and failures in orthodox observances. The homely details of the life and conversation of Jesus' (Jeshua's) Jewish family sharply contrast with the next vision, where the writer finds himself in an elaborate, costly church honoring a madonna dressed in clothes worth millions of lira.

A series of visions follows, showing the history of the church —specifically, the growth of the cult of Mary and the bloody persecutions of heretics; finally, the Jewish mother who appeared at the *Seder* meal in the first vision reappears, this time being dragged to the pyre during the burning of Jews in the Christian city of Siena. Throughout the essay Zangwill juxtaposes the vision of the worn, graying, olive-eyed Jewess with the magnificent madonna worshipped by people who would have killed the humble Jewish mother. Zangwill concludes that the carpenter's wife was transformed to suit "popular need"; but, in the transformation, Zangwill suggests, her humanity was lost.

A series of four essays develops Zangwill's humanistic philosophy. In "The Earth the Center of the Universe: Or the Absurdity of Astronomy," Zangwill argues that scientific truth is superseded by poetic vision and by the moral life. Man is, he says, the center of the universe; for, "Where the highest life is being lived, there is the center of the world, and . . . of the universe."[13] Furthermore, scientific truth (e.g., an analysis of the moon's surface) is no truer than the poet's truth (e.g., a vision of the moon's beauty). Beginning with the relativistic generalization that "all views depend on the point at which you place yourself," Zangwill develops a theory of the autocosm, defined as the individual's cosmos. Each individual has an autocosm which he constantly attempts to adjust to his experience and, if he is wise, to the macrocosm, for "Only by living in the macrocosm itself can you avoid the stern surprises which await those who snuggle into autocosm" (107).

For example, if a person relies on prayer instead of sanitation, he may be destroyed by plague; however, "it may be better to live without sanitation . . . and to die at forty of the plague . . . after years of belief in your saint or your star, than to live a century without God in a bleak universe of mechanical law" (108). In other words, Zangwill says that a faith in man and God is so desirable that even a false faith is better than no faith; but a faith that is adapted to the macrocosm is better than one which is in conflict with it. The title of the essay in which this argument appears—"Of Autocosms without Facts: Or the Emptiness of Religions"—indicates Zangwill's criticism of organized religions. The next essay, "Of Facts without Autocosms: Or the Irrelevancy of Science," says that modern science, like religion, is incomplete. Science classifies and analyzes, but it leaves the mystery of the universe unexplained; to Zangwill, the universe is "a breathing, flying, singing, striving and suffering process" (130) that is more truthfully perceived by the poet, who sees with both soul and brain.

The essay entitled "Of Facts with Alien Autocosms: Or the Futility of Culture," develops at length the art theory expressed earlier in "Men, Women and Books" and "Without Prejudice." Once again Zangwill objects to a Pater-influenced search for beauty as "hollow fantasy." He says that only with difficulty can the individual "lose the artistic Ego" in contemplating an alien autocosm (such as is represented in a work of art); and, if he does, the appreciation is only a "by-product" of art and should not be mistaken "for central verities" (141). Attacking the doctrine of art for art's sake, Zangwill suggests that every artist desires "to act—massively or diffusively—upon the life of his age"; when his art is reduced to "inactive beauty," part of "the full reality" of the work as the artist created it is lost (143). According to Zangwill, the art-for-art's-sake man misses "that wild-strawberry flavor of living, that dog-rose aroma of reality" (144).

As before, Zangwill insists on the largeness of reality and on the necessity of art to capture the "sense of life" by reconciling "the Puritan antithesis of Truth and Art, Reality and Make-Believe, Hebraism and Hellenism" (150). In the essay "Napoleon and Byron in Italy: Or Letters and Action," he says that the artist must be both doer and dreamer, arguing that the "sanest souls" combine art and feeling with power of action: "the poet who has never acted on the stage of affairs is moving in a padded world of words, and the hero who has never sung, or at least thrilled with the music in him, is only subhuman. The divorce of life and letters tends to sterilise letters and to brutalize life" (364).

*Italian Fantasies* also contains Zangwill's comments on the need for economic reform, for moral leadership, for equal rights for women, for a sense of world community to replace nationalism.[14] "The Gay Doges: Or the Failure of Society and the Impossibility of Socialism" contains Zangwill's comments on economic systems which fail. The palace of the doges of Venice and fragments of their slave galleys inspire an essay on the "defective moral sympathies" which magnificence connotes. Zangwill sees in a gilded car which is dirty white inside a "symbol of civilization"; he calls for a society in which the "State-Galley" has cars of "red and gold from blade to handle, and every man shall take his turn at them" (182). However, Zangwill does not advocate equal distribution of wealth, and he rejects the materialistic basis of Marxism. He says that "It is no evil that one man should live in a palace and another in a cottage; these differences even add to the colour and joy of life. The evil is solely that any man willing to work should lack a cottage, or that the cottage should be a malarious hovel. Levelling up is the only reform necessary, as it is the only reform possible" (186). He denies that property is one of "the essential values of life"; he maintains that "Society is sacred, not Property" (188).

To lead society, Zangwill hopes for ethical men or, society failing to produce these, at least honest men. In "The Superman of Letters: Or the Hypocrisy of Politics" Zangwill finds in a Florentine monument to Machiavelli an occasion for comments on the nature of leadership. According to Zangwill, Machiavelli was right to refuse to justify tyranny on moral grounds. As long as society substitutes expediency for morality, we should "talk of politics like Machiavelli or for ever hold our peace" (203). Machiavelli failed, however, to take into account rulers such as Moses or Buddha, whose only desire was to serve. Zangwill places his hope in the evolution of future moral leadership—the Superman—though he denies that the Superman can be deliberately bred. The other hope for moral leadership he finds in womankind. "St. Giulia and Female Suffrage" praises the modern Saint Giulias, the Suffragettes, "in revolt against a social order founded on prostitution and sex-inequality" and in pursuit of a "nobler society" (337).

### III  Essays on Nationalism, Internationalism, and the Jewish Problem

The evils of nationalism was one of Zangwill's most persistent themes; and, during and after World War I, most of his artistic energies were directed to decrying the nationalism which he felt was destroying the world. In *Italian Fantasies* he attacks the "disease" of nationalism, calling for an "Intensive Imperialism" based on brotherhood and love and producing "the highest life per square mile" (400-401). In "The Gods of Germany" (*The War for the World,* 1916), he attacks superpatriotism, a nationalism so intense that we "worship each our own national spirit, to the exclusion even of whatever God transcends humanity."[15] He develops a similar idea in *The Principle of Nationalities* (1917), where he says that nationality has become God and replaced Christianity. Admitting the difficulty of defining nationality, Zangwill says that men are more accurately divided "into first-class and third-class passengers" than into national types. He finally pleads for men to realize "their common humanity" and "to maintain the virtues of tribalism without losing the wider vision."[16]

The replacement of humane ideals by national goals led, Zangwill believes, to the disaster of World War I. In *The War for the World* Zangwill analyzes the world struggle that he had dramatized in *The War God* (1911). The title of the collection of essays means that conflicting forces struggle for control of the world and that, in a changing world, especially one at war, "no liberty is so old-established as to be safe." Zangwill is objecting specifically to the wartime Defence of the Realm Act, which threatened traditional freedoms in England. In the opening essay of the volume, he accuses England of a "growing passion for Prussianism" in suppressing plays and books. In a climate of wartime fear and suspicion, he maintains, England "has temporarily ceased to exist" (23). His fear is that the war and war politics will destroy the very liberties that the war is supposed to safeguard.

In analyzing causes for World War I, Zangwill criticizes not only nationalistic fervor but also "The Levity of War Politics"; in an essay by that name, he comments on the absurdity of international diplomacy which would "gamble with the lives and resources of generations because forsooth diplomatic dignity or Machiavellian prudence requires that neither side shall make a move toward conciliation" (202). Finally, he blames not only this war but all war on man's inherent cruelty. "The Next War" rejects the idea that World War I is a "war to end war"; in an extremely pessimistic enumeration of the many failures that lead to war, Zangwill concludes that war is inevitable until men cease being brutes. In other essays of *The War for the World,* Zangwill discusses the madness that overcomes a nation at war. For example, he laments the ruthlessness that has swept over the people demanding the total destruction of Germany.[17] Citing historian Jean de Bloch, Zangwill says that, given modern weapons and trench warfare, a decisive military victory is impossible. Furthermore, Zangwill says, such a victory would be undesirable: "It is not our business to exterminate even German militarism, much less Germany. . . . To impose *our* Kultur on her would be to do exactly what we accuse her of desiring to do with other nations. Our business is simply to see that she does not impose her *Kultur* on us whether by conquest or infection. And this business it is by no means certain we are altogether minding" (63).

In "The Ruined Romantics," referring to the Kipling-Henley school glorifying battle and empire, Zangwill attacks both the Romantics and the vested interests which, "incredible as it sounds —would rather see profit than Peace."[18] In addition to the political and economic forces favorable to war is the church, which sanctioned both sides. Zangwill summarizes his attitude toward the church's role in the war by quoting the dean of Saint Paul's: "It is nonsense to talk of the failure of Christianity when Christianity has never been tried" (266). Until the rebirth of genuine religion, until the world turns to the God of reason and love, Europe will remain in the power of the "War Devil," placing its faith in armaments, defense budgets, and fear.[19]

Though Zangwill denounced England's militaristic fervor and the loss of humane values during World War I, he was no Germanophile, as he was sometimes accused of being. In "On Catching Up a Lie" the lie is that "The true British patriot must assert that the German gray is jet-black and the British Grey snow-white"; in regard to doing so, he answers: "I fear color-blindness is not my forte" (252). He consistently defended England over Germany because England "represents a freer and less selfish civilization" (155), but he spoke out when he found England in danger of losing sight of that civilization.

Those essays in *The War for the World* which are not on the war are on the Suffragette movement or on Russia and the Jewish question. Zangwill sees the world struggle as three-fold; encompassing all struggles is the European war, while at the same time women are fighting for equality and minority groups are struggling for equal rights. "The Awkward Age of the Women's Movement" and "The Militant Suffragists" urge Suffragettes not to resort to violence but to continue to use nonviolent protest. "The War and the Women" discusses the wartime transformation of women into workers capable of doing men's jobs; therefore, "Wake Up, Parliament" (written 1915) asks for immediate granting of woman suffrage. The final essays in the book reject the romanticizing of Russia by England, especially by apologists such as Stephen Graham, who was insisting that Russia does not mistreat her Jewish populace. Graham painted a "rosy" picture of Russia; Zangwill says (in "Rosy Russia") that it is instead blood-red from its pogroms. He urges equal rights for minorities everywhere, and he believes that England is wrong not to interfere with nations such as Russia who persecute minority groups. Instead of ignoring the faults of an ally, England should be demanding that those faults be remedied.

The question of what to do about the persecution of world Jewry is the subject of Zangwill's last collection of essays, *The Voice of Jerusalem* (1920). It was a subject about which Zangwill had written all his life: his best fiction treated it; his problem dramas alluded to it; his essays and speeches frequently dwelled on it. His work with Herzl and the Jewish Territorial Organization made him a prominent figure in the Zionist movement. Though the validity of his opinions about Palestine and Zionism may still be debatable, the fact that he spent most of his life seeking an answer to the problem of Jewish homelessness and protesting the mistreatment of Jews throughout the world is not.

Commentators on Zangwill's opinions about world Jewry often stress the ambivalence which he felt toward Judaism. It is true that in *Children of the Ghetto*, as well as in Zangwill's personal life, there is a pulling away from orthodox Judaism. But it is also true that from his earliest works he recognized in Judaism a morality capable of leading the world, and in this opinion he wavered little during his lifetime. One of his early essays, "The Position of Judaism" (1895), speaks of the failure of Christianity because of its otherworldliness to answer the needs of modern man; on the other hand, Judaism, with its acceptance of the sensuous world (in fact, its ability to make religion relevant to virtually every facet of life in that world), its emphasis on family and community, and its tendency "to unification" is peculiarly suited to the modern spirit. The essay defines the position of Judaism (the "original Catholic Democratic Church of Humanity") and the mission of Israel (to bring "its own moral vision to the world").[20]

This vision, *The Voice of Jerusalem* tells us, is that of "a righteous social order, and an ultimate unification of mankind" (9). As before, Zangwill comments on the failure of Christianity, with a world war as well as pogroms in Poland and Russia as proof of it. He feels that the Jews are the only people left with an ideal of "the unity of the universe, . . . the brotherhood of humanity under the common fatherhood, and . . . a warless world" (12). It is not so much that Jews are "spiritual supermen" as that other stocks are "subhuman";[21] such groups accept atrocities in war as normal, wage savage purges, fail to restore Europe after the war to economic and political health, continue the system of national alliances that led to World War I—in short, they lack reason and love.

*The Voice of Jerusalem* falls into three parts: the first analyzing the nature of Jews, Judaism, and the ghetto; the second, Zionism and the failure of the world to give the Jews a home; the third, the failure of the world to achieve commonwealth. All are unified by the idea that the voice of Jerusalem is a voice of reason and love, a call to brotherhood and unity. The first section gives, in addition to a definition of Judaism's mission, a detailed analysis of ghetto life. Reminding us once more that reality has elements of romance in it, Zangwill criticizes portrayals of the Jew which, though avoiding the grotesque figure of legend, present only a prosaic figure in his place. The ghetto, as Zangwill sees it, was gross and ugly; but it also had "boundless aspects of romance and tragedy" and, above all, a "desperate will-to-live" (28).

Illustrating this will, Zangwill contrasts the Jewish ghetto with the Christian slum, noting that the Sidney Webbs's description of the sordid lives of the poor was unfamiliar to him, who had grown up in the Whitechapel ghetto. According to Zangwill, people are destroyed not by lack of wealth but "for lack of vision or for overplus of false vision"; to the children of the ghetto, Judaism provided the vision that added poetry to an otherwise miserable life. The ritual of Judaism was "not *added* to life" but *was* life; thus every day was transformed from a sordid struggle for existence into a sanctified "domestic ritual of singular beauty and poetry and tender and self-controlling traits of character" (34). Contrary to fictional and sociological descriptions of slum life, Zangwill says that in the ghetto he had "in no instance seen personality destroyed

or degraded, but in numberless instances accentuated and up-
lifted" (29).

In the second section of the book, Zangwill traces the history
of Zionism, with reference to his part in that movement. Up to
the present, he says, Zionism has always been "a shadowy, poetic
idea" and the Jews a race of nomads, with Scripture substituting
for territory. If, in the past, Christians had believed in brotherhood
and love, European Jewry might have been assimilated into the
Christian world; but instead, Christians persecuted Jews, who were
thus held together by adversity. Now the Jews want their own
homeland, and they await Palestine (78–79). Zangwill hopes
that Zionism will not become nationalism but will continue to
mean a striving for world brotherhood. However, he admits that
the Jews must have a nation; for Israel talking brotherhood without a home "is like a *Schnorrer* [beggar] talking socialism" (89).

Earlier Zangwill had broken from the Zionists to form the
Jewish Territorial Organization, which was dedicated to finding a
Jewish homeland anywhere in the world and to rejecting the
desire for Palestine as too unrealistic. After the Balfour Declaration of 1917, he for a while favored Palestine as a Jewish homeland, advocating British rule, population redistribution, and com-
pensation for expropriated Arab land. However, he decided that
England had mishandled the Palestine situation, creating British
rule and an Arab majority, so that Palestine "is neither Jewish
nor National nor a Home." Thus Zangwill turned again to his old
position, and in 1923 he delivered his famous "Watchman, What
of the Night?" speech, in which he declared that political Zionism
was dead. For this opinion he was reviled by American Jewry and
opposed by many British Jews. The sad fact is that a man who
spent most of his life writing about and working for his people
was at the end rejected by many of them. His views on Palestine
were understandably unpopular; in retrospect, we can say that he
was wrong about the death of political Zionism, but it is by no
means certain that he was wrong about the problems inherent in
designating Palestine the Jewish homeland.

To Zangwill, the fact that Jews needed a nation was itself a
comment on the failure of the Christian world. Zangwill would
have preferred that Europe learn to respect and protect minorities;
but after World War I, he was convinced that the world had not
and would not oppose oppression. In support of this thesis, the

last section of *The Voice of Jerusalem* criticizes "the fiasco" of the League of Nations and the continuing failure of international politics. Zangwill found Europe still filled with "insane imperialisms," and he believed the League was destined to fail because nations were excluded, allowed to withdraw, and given to revenge. Europe, he says, ended " 'the war against war' by a Peace against Peace" (128). Ideally, politics would grow out of a religious spirit of world kinship and community, but Zangwill saw no evidence of that spirit in the postwar political scene. *The Voice of Jerusalem* ends with a bleak prediction: "But humanity has not suffered enough, and doubtless we have to undergo still grimmer experiences before our almost incorrigible hearts are chastened, and our gun-deafened ears turned and attuned to the still small voice of Jerusalem" (136).

The Zangwill of this passage seems a different man from the clever wit writing items for "The Idlers' Club" in 1892: one is an entertainer; the other, a prophet. However, the seeds of the later seriousness are in Zangwill's earliest work, notably in his ghetto fiction and in his social criticism of the 1890's. If his essays ceased to entertain as he turned his attention to Zionism, war politics, and programs of world community, they show no loss of literary power. In fact, the early, trivial essays now seem most dated in ideas and technique; but the social criticism remains interesting and effective.

# CHAPTER 3

# *Ridicule, Reality, and Romance: Zangwill's Novels*

Z angwill began his career as novelist early. In "My First
Book" Zangwill says that when he was ten he wrote a
"romance of school life in two volumes . . . in a couple of exercise
books"; and, when he was sixteen, he received "honorable mention" for a story submitted to a prize competition sponsored by
the weekly *Society*.[1] These earliest works apparently fore-
shadowed the New Humor with which Zangwill was first popularly
associated, for the copybook romance dealt "with teacher-baiting
tricks" and the contribution to *Society* won in the "humorous
story" category of the contest.

Zangwill's earliest published novels were a political satire, *The
Premier and the Painter* (1888), and two humorous works, *The
Bachelors' Club* (1891) and *The Old Maids' Club* (1892). These
early works show promise but suffer from a self-conscious display
of wit, overabundant detail, and a labored style. Though Zangwill
began as a humorist, he soon moved to the serio-comic (or tragi-
comic) view characteristic of his best work, such as *Children of the
Ghetto* (1892) and *The King of Schnorrers* (1894). Of his other
novels, *The Master* (1895) deserves a place among the "portrait
of the artist" stories at the end of the century, but *The Mantle of
Elijah* (1900), an attack on modern politics, is best forgotten.
Toward the end of a long career as novelist, short-story writer,
dramatist, poet, and essayist, Zangwill produced his last novel,
*Jinny the Carrier* (1919), which deliberately escapes from the
twentieth century by turning to a subject and technique of an
earlier and simpler day.

## I   The Premier and the Painter

*The Premier and the Painter* was written in collaboration with
Louis Cowen, a fellow teacher at the Jews' Free School, and published by Spencer Blackett in 1888 under the pseudonym "J. Free-

man Bell." According to Zangwill's account of the book's genesis, Cowen proposed a book in which "a Radical Prime Minister and a Conservative working man should change into each other by supernatural means"; Zangwill, who altered the plan, makes the transformation realistic, not supernatural, and changes the politics of each. The resulting work, written almost entirely by Zangwill, is a satiric analysis of English politics, deserving Zangwill's description of it as both "A Fantastic Romance" and a "political treatise." [2]

The theme of political disorder is introduced in the opening words of the book, for a newsboy shouts news of dissension in the premier's cabinet. In the opening chapter, Conservative premier Arnold Floppington (popularly called "Floppy") finds his double in a Radical working man, a sign painter, Jack Dawe. By the end of the chapter, the two have changed places; and the rest of the book depicts the results of this change by contrasting the character of the self-assured, dynamic, but Philistine painter turned premier with that of the philosophical, indecisive, but moral premier turned painter. Ironically, the sign painter is an eminently successful politician, and the premier is a failure not only in politics but also in work and in love. In his brief career as premier, Jack Dawe stops dissension in the cabinet, averts a threatened dissolution of the government, achieves the enfranchisement of women, and introduces a bill supporting Irish Home Rule. On the other hand, Arnold Floppington ruins Dawe's sign-painting business, causes him to be sued for breach of promise, and fails to stop his assassination even though he knows that the premier's life is in danger. Finally, the real premier returns to power, without the country's ever knowing of the exchange of roles that had taken place.

Structurally, *The Premier and the Painter* depends on the contrast in character of the two men and on the balancing of two love triangles. The character contrast is clear from the beginning: Floppington is first seen walking abstractedly through Bethnal Green, where he wanders aimlessly into a meeting of a workingmen's debating club; Dawe is delivering at this club a forceful denunciation of "Floppy" and the Conservative government. After the two men change roles, the premier (now Dawe) shows an increase in physical vigor, begins reading Radical newspapers, outwits his rival in politics and love, and generally displays greater decisiveness, wit, and political acumen than Floppington had. The sign painter (now Floppington) becomes reflective, meek, and given to illness. He shocks his belligerently atheistic old mother by going to church and discussing theology with the vicar. And he seems unsuited for even the simplest tasks: of the art of sign painting he knows nothing; and, in one hilarious chapter (Book II, Chapter 2), he paints an unrecognizable red lion on a signboard while reciting Aeschylus to a vastly amused crowd of onlookers. When he has to assist his mother in her cookshop, his inability even to serve meals causes him to reflect, accurately, "I am unfitted for whatever part I undertake to play." [3]

*The Premier and the Painter* presents a pessimistic view of human nature: the well-intentioned, kindhearted Floppington is unsuited for a world which is too corrupt for him to cope with; and the aggressive, ruthless, worldly wise Dawe, eminently suited to rule, can never, except by a subterfuge, achieve ruling power. At one point in the novel (Bk. IV, Chs. 4–9), the two return to their "natural" roles; and Dawe discovers his household in disorder and his reputation ruined. Despairing, he reflects that "Life is no fairy tale, but a cruel comedy of errors, a muddle where the fools have seized upon the duties meant for the wise, and the wise have been thrust into the places of the fools, and, unkindest cut of all! they have got so rooted into their surroundings, that an attempt to change places must bring unhappiness to both" (237). Dawe, of course, sees himself as one of the wise and Floppington as the fool, but their characters are not so simple. Dawe's wisdom is of the world; Floppy's, of the spirit. And the folly of both men is caused by their being thrust into roles not in keeping with their natural inclinations. In an absurd society the man of action is denied power, and the man of thought is forced to act.

The two love stories which complicate the plot involve Floppington, who is in love with Lady Gwendolyn Harley, and Dawe, who is trying to extricate himself from his commitment to a housemaid, Eliza Bathbrill. When Floppington poses as Dawe, he cannot bear to hurt Eliza's feelings and promises to marry her; at the same time, his gentleness causes his mother's serving girl, Sally, to fall in love with him (as Dawe). Both Floppington's and Dawe's romances go awry: Eliza coincidentally becomes a housemaid for Lady Gwendolyn and recognizes Dawe (posing as Floppy) at Lady Gwendolyn's; then Lady Gwendolyn, believing that Floppington has seduced her housemaid, accepts another man. And Eliza, having lost interest in Dawe (Floppington), breaks off their engagement; but she sues him for breach of promise when she discovers that he is not heartbroken. Both love stories are resolved after Dawe's assassination and Floppington's return to the premiership: Eliza marries a new lover; Sally, inspired by Dawe's (Floppy's) spiritual example, educates herself and becomes a teacher; Lady Gwendolyn learns the truth about the exchange of roles and marries Floppy.

*The Premier and the Painter* is divided into seven books. In the first chapter of Book I, Floppington and Dawe change roles; in the closing two chapters of Book VII, Floppington resumes his role as premier. Between these opening and closing chapters there are sections dealing alternately with the careers of Dawe and Floppington. This alternation is carefully controlled in the opening books: after the change, Book I devotes two chapters (2 and 3) to Jack Dawe and the remaining chapters (4-8) to Floppington; then all of Book II concerns Dawe, and all of Book III concerns Floppington. In Book IV, exactly midway through the entire work, the men return briefly (Chs. 4–9) to their former roles, with disastrous results to Floppington's romance and to Dawe's faith in humanity. Books V and VI are less regular in design, though Zangwill continues alternately focusing on events in the two men's lives. Book V moves into the improbabilities of melodrama, as Dawe (Floppy) accidentally falls into a den of conspirators who are planning the assassination of the premier unless he abandons his support of Irish Home Rule. Book VI ends as Floppington (Dawe) delivers a brilliant speech in support of Home Rule, a speech which is his last; and Dawe (Floppy), his life unbelievably complicated by Eliza's devotion, bids a last farewell to Mrs. Dawe's cookshop. Book VII depicts the national confusion over the assassination of the prime minister, with the confusion finally stopped by Floppy's reappearance. The entire work focuses on the philosophic Floppington, who is the central character of the book; for he receives twenty-eight chapters to Dawe's eighteen. Dawe disappears entirely in Book VII, when our attention is directed to Floppy's regaining the esteem of Lady Gwendolyn and the control of his party.

One of the book's most startling characteristics is its length; a contemporary critic, complaining of its inordinate length, asserted that "probably no human being could read, without generous omissions, its five hundred closely printed pages." [4] The critic was wrong about the possibility of such human effort, but he was right to complain about the excessive length of the book. However, if we are willing to make the effort, we discover that the next most startling characteristic of the work is the range and potency of its satire. Having conceived the device of putting a Radical worker at the head of the Tory aristocracy, Zangwill found a rich vein of satire open to him. He shows us the chameleon politician who will propose or reject legislation as it suits his personal purposes. He depicts the Conservative's justification for introducing Radical reforms: "The changes we bring about are improvements, those brought about by Radicals are revolutions" (119). He creates conspirators hired by the Irish to defeat Home Rule on the grounds that it would rob the Irish of their dearest national possession—hatred of the English. He satirically glances at the fashionable world of art and letters, at the unscrupulous woman who wants out of her engagement but not without causing pain, at the brutality and intolerance of the poor and uneducated. In the last book, he ridicules the fact-finding bodies of government: after Premier Dawe's death, a coroner's inquest is held, evidence is painstakingly gathered, testimony is heard, the proceedings are summarized, and a jury returns a verdict that reverses the truth. Even after Floppington returns, the government and the newspapers never learn the truth but settle for another garbled account of what really happened.

The book has superb comic touches. Mrs. Dawe, forever copiously quoting her freethinking husband and horrified by her son's sudden turn toward religion, is a memorable comic character, as is the "Social Socialist" of Book IV, Chapter 12, who sociably explains his politics to Dawe while stealing his purse. A farcical scene occurs when Jack Dawe returns home (Bk. IV, Ch. 7) to find his household in total disorder, Eliza expecting marriage, Sally impudent and possessive, his mother apparently dead, and an undertaker complaining of social reforms that are wrecking his business. When Mrs. Dawe revives to hear them discussing her burial, chaos ensues in a riotously confused scene. Much of the comedy in the novel arises from the naïve Floppington's utter incompetence in the workaday world, as in his Aeschylus-reciting sign-painting attempt (Bk. II, Ch. 2), or in his expression of shock that Reform Laws are violated (Bk. IV, Ch. 11), or in his encounter with a little ragged child, "an image of purity and innocence," whom he envisions brightening the home of her poor parents (Bk. IV, Ch. 13). In the latter episode, Floppy (as Dawe), touched by the child, offers to buy her a new pair of shoes; he then discovers that his money has been stolen and invites the child to his house for the money. At this point, a policeman interrupts with "Now what little game are you up to, eh?" The result of the well-meaning Floppy's offer is that he barely escapes arrest on suspicion of perversion, and the child is beaten by its parents for being late with the beer for supper.

The humor of *The Premier and the Painter* derives not only from this ironic, often grim, humor but also from literary parodies. John Ruskin's style is parodied when, apropos of Dawe's sign painting, Zangwill quotes from " 'Modern-Sign-Painters,' Vol. VI, pp. 35–36." Book VII parodies journalistic misrepresentations of the news, a favorite object of ridicule throughout the work. Part of the humor of *The Premier and the Painter* is Zangwill's pretense, despite wild improbabilities and stylistic extravagances, that he is writing history, not romance or melodrama. The Preface to the first edition states soberly that "the present work is simply a *novel* method of writing history, and . . . real personages and real events are for the first time treated with the fulness of domestic and political detail hitherto accorded only to the creations of fiction." Scholarly footnotes and overt reminders in the narrative keep up the pretense. For example, when Dawe is with the Irish conspirators, Zangwill interrupts the narrative to apologize for being unable to let Dawe heroically extricate himself from his difficulties: "It is at this point that the present historian for the first time regrets his office, and envies the more brilliant functions of the novelist, and it is only the consoling reflection that his labours are more likely to be durable that induces him to proceed with so comparatively tame a narration. Unable to choose his hero, or at least, to change him when chosen, he is compelled to see him wasting the most sensational opportunities, and he cannot stir a finger while his best chapters are spoiled by the demands of a dull veracity" (319–320). Zangwill then admits that the scene is straight out of melodrama but that his hero is not.

Such intrusions of the author into the narrative occur often.

The style is that of an earnest historian stopping occasionally to say, "Imagine, therefore, dear reader, that . . ." or, "While he is rolling homewards we shall have time to point a moral . . ." (54, 222). Occasionally, the historian becomes rhapsodic; but most of the time he employs a serviceable but not distinguished prose, the faults of which must be attributed to early Zangwill, not to a persona. The major faults of the writing, as one critic has noted, are "garrulity and riotous diction."[5] And painful examples of this blemish are "The unwonted carmine overspread her face and neck" (11); "Dogs, preceded by their tongues, strolled languidly along. . . . It was just noon, and thirst reigned supreme" (74); "Eliza assumed an air of impenetrable hauteur, but Sally, preserving the contour of a two-handled vase, sent her a saucy leer" (261).

Such examples, though too frequent, are, however, not typical of the style. Zangwill was apparently aware of the faults of the youthful work, and in a Preface "For the Gentle American Reader" (1896) he says that, as "a shy youth writing his first book," he drew a character "in words which I knew well at the time constituted a candid criticism of myself and my own book. 'He had signalised himself and his ignorance by writing a flippant satire on everything under the sun in the form of a political burlesque, and his shyness in society was only equalled by his audacity on paper.' "[6]

In another Preface (to the Third Edition), Zangwill acknowledges the literary source of *The Premier and the Painter*, noting that "History has plagiarised from a romance conceived nearly a decade ago." The reference is to Mark Twain's *The Prince and the Pauper* (1881), which has more in common with Zangwill's historical "romance" than the alliterative title. The central motif, the exchange of roles, is obviously borrowed from Twain's novel in which a slum child changes places with the Prince of Wales; Twain's Offal Court out of Pudding Lane becomes Zangwill's Bethnal Green in Whitechapel; Twain's child of the slum, Tom Canty, like Zangwill's Radical workingman, Jack Dawe, is an avid reader and a natural leader, looked up to by his comrades "as a superior being" (Ch. 2). Tom's mother, like Dawe's mother, is convinced that her son (actually, the prince) has lost his wits because of his "foolish reading"; Mrs. Dawe is convinced that Jack (actually, the premier) has gone mad because of his preoccupation with politics. When Tom becomes prince, he rules England mercifully, destroying cruel and oppressive laws (Ch. 27), just as Dawe as premier institutes reform legislation.

The plots of both Zangwill and Twain follow the plan of alternately presenting the adventures of each character, with the final exchange of roles made before a huge crowd: the prince resumes his place on coronation day; the premier, in Parliament on the day of Dawe's funeral. Both books are heavily satiric, Twain's focusing on the fierce and unjust punishment for minor theft or religious unorthodoxy in late sixteenth-century England. Zangwill probably borrowed the idea of pretending to write history from Twain's book, which also uses authentic historical detail—even footnotes—to describe the pageantry of the king's life and the horror of the pauper's.

Of course, Zangwill made modifications in his source—several hundred pages of them, in fact. He wisely omitted the sentimental subplot of *The Prince and the Pauper,* in which Miles Hendon, the befriender of the pauper-king, is restored to his inheritance and his true love, both stolen from him by a wicked younger brother. Zangwill also avoided Twain's sentimental attitude toward women; for example, Tom Canty's patient, long-suffering mother becomes the aggressive, loquacious Mrs. Dawe. Zangwill also modified the complication of the plot, making the exchange of roles deliberate, whereas the prince and the pauper accidentally change places. He also modified the conclusion: Twain's prince learns how to rule better from his experience in the slums and in prison; Zangwill's Floppy is still ineffectual when he returns to power, and eventually retires to lead a happier life away from the public eye. To summarize, Zangwill's *Premier and the Painter* is less sentimental, more consistently satiric, less assured of a happy ending than its source.

## II  The Celibates' Club

In spite of its merits—and they overshadow its faults—*The Premier and the Painter* was not a popular success; but success arrived with Zangwill's next book. With the publication of *The Bachelors' Club* (1891), Zangwill says, "I crossed Fleet Street and stepped into what is called 'success.' "[7] *The Bachelors' Club* was followed in 1892 by *The Old Maids' Club,* and both works

were collected to form *The Celibates' Club* in 1898. Both are
exercises in playful irony concerning the adventures of miscellaneous individuals united by a common purpose—to remain
single. The form is a series of sketches, and the pattern followed
in narrative is similar: in *The Bachelors' Club,* the fall from grace
of one bachelor after another; in *The Old Maids' Club,* the failure
of successive candidates to qualify as old maids.

*The Bachelors' Club* consists of a Prologue and thirteen chapters. The Prologue explains the nature of the club, the rules for
admission of members and visitors, and the club's dogmas; it
introduces the twelve members, including the appropriately named
narrator, Paul Pry. The last pages of the Prologue narrate how
Pry came to be elected to membership; he was a replacement for
Willoughby Jones, whose marriage expelled him from the club,
but who returned, repentant, as a club waiter. The Prologue ends,
"From that day to this no member of the Bachelors' Club has
ever cherished the grand passion";[8] then the rest of the book
recounts, with one chapter for each member, how each violated
the basic rule of "Do not marry." The book is unified not only
by the devotion of all the principal characters to a common ideal
but also by the appearance of Pry in all the tales and by the
structural similarity of all of them.

In each tale, the bachelor is first characterized—his background, his present situation, and his peculiarities; then he is
confronted by a problem, which demands for its solution his
marriage; finally, a short epilogue states the ironic outcome of
the marriage. The first chapter, entitled "The Second Ticket,"
exemplifies this structure: Osmund Bethel, after a poverty-stricken
childhood, followed by a struggle to succeed as a journalist, becomes a drama critic for *Whirlpool;* when he becomes well
known, theaters begin to send him two complimentary passes to
performances. His frugality prompts him not to waste the extra
ticket, and he is distracted by the problem of finding someone to
share his ticket. Finally, he becomes engaged so that he can stop
worrying about what to do with the second ticket. He explains
his decision to Paul Pry: "I don't wish to marry the girl: only
to be engaged to her, so that she may accompany me. I would
willingly remain engaged to her for ever, but the narrow vision
of society . . . sees only one issue to engagement—and that is
marriage. I will take her regularly to the play. . . . And when she

insists upon it, I shall marry her" (23). So Bethel marries, and
an epilogue concludes: "The *Whirlpool's* leap upwards was but
a spasm. It did not remain a waterspout long. . . . The acting-
managers send it only one ticket now" (24).

The other tales follow this pattern. One bachelor marries his
faithful old housekeeper, whose ugliness is surpassed only by her
bad cooking, so that he can hire a cook and get a decent meal;
another marries on his way out of England to avoid breaking a
fearful oath not to marry while he is abroad; another marries as
a result of a lifelong love for a mnemonic form called "Barbara";
another, to prove his theory that one cannot marry on three hundred pounds a year; and so it goes, until every bachelor is married. In the climactic chapter, Pry discovers that the president
of the club, M'Gullicuddy, is in fact a bigamist; to escape his
second wife, M'Gullicuddy founded the club as the least likely
place for a bigamist to be found. In the final chapter, the disillusioned Pry marries and bids a "sad farewell" to all the old faces.

Each of the chapters, except Chapter 5, tells the story of one
bachelor and his marriage. Chapter 5 depicts a club banquet and
after dinner meeting at which members read papers and the secretary reads biographical sketches of new candidates for the rapidly
decreasing membership of the club. This chapter functions primarily as the occasion for Zangwill's inclusion of clever papers
and humorous sketches about miscellaneous subjects, and it was
wisely omitted in his revision of *The Bachelors' Club*. In the version for *The Celibates' Club,* there are twelve chapters, one for
each of the twelve members.

The tales, whimsical studies in human absurdity, ignore realistic
probability. Occasionally, a satirical intention is evident, but the
satire is never harsh. A number of the tales satirize the literary
world, enough so that criticism of the follies of that world constitutes a minor theme of the book. For example, Chapter 3, "Hamlet
Up to Date," attacks authors who build a reputation on the basis
of another man's writing. In a story within a story about a modern
Hamlet who sees a ghost writer instead of a ghost, a bachelor
exposes his novelist father's fraud; and, to compensate for his
father's neglect of the ghost, he marries the ghost's daughter. "The
Fall of Israfel" parodies the soulful esthetic poet who charms
drawing-room society with his ballads and satirizes an artistically
ignorant public, which cannot tell a burlesque song from a serious

ballad. Zangwill specifically parodies Algernon Charles Swinburne in Israfel's song to the Bachelor's Club (124), which begins, "O fly with me where amaranthine blossoms/ Are pale with passion's flame,/ Where larger moons and lither-limb'd opossums/ Know naught of sin and shame." "A Novel Advertisement" satirizes both the charlatanism of critics and the narrative ineptitude of authors. Bachelor O'Roherty is depressed because his ironically named book, *A Summer Idyll,* a "sordid tragi-comedy centred around Camberwell Green," has received critical praise for its "pretty pastoral story." O'Roherty is also having difficulties with writing: he complains that he is only good at "plot, character-drawing, real human dialogue" and thus cannot write a modern novel. In this tale Zangwill attacks a novelistic art which thrives on everything except the traditional matter of narrative. The narrator of *The Bachelors' Club,* Paul Pry, is also a literary man. Pry starts a paper specializing in interviews and in the first issue features a writer who insists that "There never was an age in which so many people were able to write badly" (266). When the interview paper fails, Pry decides to start a humorous paper which will avoid triteness by avoiding jokes about mothers-in-law and drunks. Rationalizing that he must "save English humor," Pry marries the lovely daughter of a charming mother, only to discover that the owner of his paper insists that he use mother-in-law jokes.

Literary satire also appears as a subtheme in *The Old Maids' Club.* This book includes a lady novelist (Andrew Didbin) whose husband must furnish a background against which her genius can shine; a Mutual Depreciation Society, composed of six men of letters who write puffs of each other but meet socially to damn each other's work and who for a joke create a famous (nonexistent) literary genius, "The English Shakespeare"; a famous female art and music critic (Frank Maddox), who refused to marry her artist-lover because "I know nothing about music or art, and I was afraid he would find me out"; and a poet, Silverplume, whose poetry is a parody of *fin de siècle* poems. *The Old Maids' Club* also contains a number of such poems by Lord Silverdale, who reads them, often with banjo accompaniment, to Lillie Dulcimer as they await new candidates for the Old Maids' Club.

The satiric range of *The Old Maids' Club* is much wider than that of *The Bachelors' Club.* In addition to the satire on the literary world is Zangwill's satire of the man who has achieved social success by doing nothing. Echoing and parodying the argument of Oscar Wilde's "The Critic as Artist" (1890), Zangwill's "Man in the Ironed Mask" says that "Inaction is perfect. . . . Only by not having done anything to deserve success can you be sure of surviving the reaction which success always brings. To be is higher than to do. To be is calm, large, elemental; to do is trivial, artificial, fussy. To be has been the moth of the English aristocracy, it is the secret of their persistence."[9] Zangwill also satirizes contemporary advertising (Ch. 5) and domestic servant-master relations (Ch. 9).

The primary target of Zangwill's satire is, however, womankind; and he includes almost every kind of woman. There is a vain actress, perversely attracted to the only man who is indifferent to her; a female novelist, whose literary aspirations supersede her love for a man; a young woman who wants a husband with a past and refuses all suitors because they swear that they have never loved before; a self-sacrificing woman, whose ethical sense makes her declare that "It would not be fair to a lover to chain him to a beauty so transient" (496); a crusading Feminist, so masculine that the butler announces her as "a gentleman who gives his name as a lady" (525); her opposite, the woman in "protest against the defeminization of my sex" who seeks an old-fashioned, thoroughly conventional husband. And there are many others—even a passionate Frenchwoman angry at the priggish propriety of her English lover and a Boston heiress in search of capsulized culture.

But the wide range of satire in this book is unfortunately at the expense of formal neatness. *The Old Maids' Club* lacks the structural control of *The Bachelors' Club*, which moves surely, chapter by chapter, to the end—the dissolution of the club. However, *The Old Maids' Club* does move inevitably, though not so precisely, to a similar end. The first two chapters depict the formation of the club by a millionaire's daughter, Lillie Dulcimer, who decides not to marry because mathematical probability says that the man she loves will not love her. In apparent earnestness, she starts the Old Maids' Club and commissions the man she loves, Lord Silverdale, to serve as "honorary trier" of all candidates. The rest of the book shows the failure of successive candidates to qualify for reasons as varied and unusual as their stories. The stories include a modern fairy tale, "The Princess on Portman Square," in which the princess sets the usual three tasks for her two suitors; an unusual mystery story involving a Spanish Catholic, who falls in love with a Jewess and tries, unsuccessfully, to "pass" as a Jew; a humorous story of a man whose romance is almost wrecked by his obsession with putting advertisements in the personal columns; an ironic tale of a selfish girl who deprives a dying stranger of his life insurance and later discovers that her fiancé was the man's heir.

In spite of the abundance of characters and stories, *The Old Maids' Club* is unified by the major conflict underlying all the stories: celibacy versus marriage. This conflict is introduced in the opening chapter as Lillie, for "logical" reasons, decides not to marry Lord Silverdale and therefore not anyone. Lillie and Lord Silverdale appear in all the chapters as listeners or tellers of the tales, and their own love story is developed in transitional sections and ends in marriage in the final chapter. In this chapter, a *real* old maid appears, an old, withered woman dressed in youthful clothes; she calls herself "Little Dolly" and comes to join the Old Maids' Club. Lillie's glimpse of the simpering, absurd, and pathetic figure causes her to "end the tragi-comedy" she is enacting and to promise to marry Lord Silverdale.

As we would expect, *The Bachelors' Club* and *The Old Maids' Club* complement each other. The theme of both is marriage; more specifically, both books suggest that no amount of rules, resolutions, and organization can or should overrule the natural inclination of man (and woman) to marry. Finally, there are no members of the Celibates' Club. In the development of this theme lies Zangwill's comic force, and the humor which is most successful involves the comic irony of would-be celibates falling before Cupid.

Less successful is the humor deriving from wordplay or inversions of maxims or clichés. We are inclined to agree when Paul Pry prefaces the not very witty Bachelors' maxims with "Here are the worst of them" (7). The puns often seemed forced: "Little Bethel they called him at the Club; not because he ever had any Methodism in his madness, but because . . ."; "The kidneys were passable, but unfortunately there was no other guest to pass them to" (13, 30). An example of more esoteric but no less labored wordplay is the description of a drunk cabman's speech as "perfect English, marred only by the little Latin expletives in the brackets" (56). In Zangwill's defense, he is aware of the wretched puns, for he has Lillie forbid them in *The Old Maids' Club* because "They spoiled the Bachelors' Club" (320).

Some of his attempts at ironic reversals are more successful; for example, Ellaline Rand (Andrew Didbin) says to her disappointed lover that an unhappy ending "is not my style, . . . but after all this is only real life"; and Lillie Dulcimer advises the girl seeking a wicked husband to try one last lover: "Otherwise you might always reproach yourself that you had perhaps turned away from a bad man's love. You might feel that the world was not so good as you had imagined in your girlish cynicism."[10] As Zangwill matured as a writer, his humor depended less on such wordplay and forced cleverness and more on the tragi-comic irony of existence; at depicting the latter, he sometimes rose to artistic greatness, as in his next book, *Children of the Ghetto.*

## III   Children of the Ghetto

*Children of the Ghetto* was published in 1892 by the newly founded Jewish Publication Society in Philadelphia, which commissioned Zangwill to write "a Jewish *Robert Elsmere.*"[11] The result was considerably more than a Jewish version of Mrs. Humphrey Ward's popular novel dealing with the problem of faith in the modern world; indeed, the strongest parts of *Children of the Ghetto* are those least influenced by *Robert Elsmere.*

*Children of the Ghetto,* set in late nineteenth-century London, is divided into two books: *Children of the Ghetto,* depicting life in the Whitechapel ghetto, and *Grandchildren of the Ghetto,* showing middle-class Jewry outside the ghetto. The first book, with its unforgettable characters set in a milieu in which traditional values are collapsing but have not yet completely done so, is superior to the second book, in which essentially flat characters are placed in discursive rather than dramatic situations.

Book I is a panorama of life in the ghetto, consisting of character sketches and stories of the struggle to survive. In depiction of character, Zangwill is free from sentimentalism and avoids the stereotype. This objectivity is evident even in his portraits of minor characters, for example, the "sweater," Bear Belcovitch. The title of Chapter 2, "The Sweater," calls up the image of a hardhearted villain prospering by overworking and underpaying his workers. Instead, we see the "sweater" at the engagement party of his daughter, where his character is that of a hard-working, affectionate, and basically generous man with a miserly temperament.

Zangwill points up the discrepancy between the popular and personal image of the "sweater": "In Parliamentary Blue-Books, English newspapers, and the Berner Street Socialistic Club, he was called a 'sweater,' and the comic papers pictured him with a protuberant paunch and a greasy smile, but he had not the remotest idea that he was other than a God-fearing, industrious, and even philanthropic citizen."[12]

In creating his characters Zangwill combines apparent objectivity with actual sympathy to produce the effect described in the Proem to *Children of the Ghetto,* where he says that "the rose of romance" can bloom "in the raw air of English reality" (ix). Just as Bear Belcovitch refutes the stereotype of the "sweater," so do other characters in *Children of the Ghetto* resist stereotyping. The dirty, shiftless peddler becomes the pious inheritor of a glorious tradition as he presides over the *Seder* table; parents who have never loved each other find romance in mutual sacrifice for their children; a confidence man is transformed into a poet and prophet of Israel. The ghetto comes alive, peopled by the "sweater," the peddler, the poet, the rabbi, the "fallen woman," the marriage broker, the business man, the labor leader, and others.

The novel abounds in scenes characteristic of ghetto life; depicted are a soup kitchen for the poor ("The Bread of Affliction," Ch. 1), a Zionist meeting ("The Holy Land League," Ch. 15), a meeting of workers on strike ("With the Strikers," Ch. 19), and a play at the Yiddish theater ("The Jargon Players," Ch. 21). Behind all the activities of the ghetto is the Jewish religion—the customs, stories, jokes, songs, and rituals of Judaism, which provide not only the background but the basis of conflict in Book I. As background, Zangwill includes almost enough exposition of Jewish tradition and ritual to justify one critic's dismissal of Zangwill as "a purveyor of exotica";[13] in fact, the major fault of Book I is the copious and extraneous recounting of Jewish jokes (90–93), Yiddish songs (106–7), and Jewish folklore (108–110).

But the even more abundant detailing of Jewish ritual serves a thematic purpose, for the resolution of the major conflict in the book relies on the emotional appeal of this ritual. During the book we witness an engagement (Ch. 7), a redemption of the son (Ch. 4), marriage and divorce (Ch. 4), a synagogue service (Ch. 12), a bar-mitzvah (Ch. 13), a funeral, and, finally, the Jewish Sabbath (Ch. 18) and *Seder* (Ch. 25).

The central conflict in *Children of the Ghetto* is that of youth versus age: specifically, of child versus parent. Zangwill finds in the break from orthodox Judaism a metaphor for this universal conflict. The children of the ghetto are beginning to doubt and distrust the religion of their fathers. Thus we find Hannah Jacobs, the daughter of a rabbi, laughing "in contemptuous amusement at the rigidity of Jewish Law" (Ch. 4); we find her deciding never to marry rather than to submit to her father's choice of a suitable match for her (Ch. 6); and finally we find her lover rejected because of the "old law." At a friend's engagement party, Hannah receives a ring and a joking pledge of marriage from the prospective bridegroom; then she learns that this joke is, according to Jewish law, a legal marriage, which can only be dissolved by divorce.

After her divorce, Hannah falls in love with David Brandon, who, like Hannah, has fallen away from orthodox Judaism; to her surprise, her father does not object to their marriage, for he reasons that David's "unborn soul undertook the yoke of the Torah at Sinae" (231); but the law intervenes to stop the marriage of Hannah and David. Her father discovers that Brandon is a *Cohen;* and, as a member of the hereditary priesthood, he cannot marry a divorcee. Hannah argues that her marriage was only a jest and that her divorce was equally meaningless, but her father allows no jesting with the Torah and forbids her marriage to David. Hannah resolves to elope with David in spite of her father's objection, but she finds herself unable to break from the *Seder* ceremony on the night of her intended elopement.

Throughout the book, Hannah, rebellious and iconoclastic, finds herself emotionally clinging to her father, the gentle, kindly "Reb" Shemuel, who literally gives the coat off his back to the needy (Ch. 6). The father is representative of both the greatness and the rigidity of orthodoxy; and he is as close to an expression of values in *Children of the Ghetto* as we can find. He is considered "a force impeding the Anglicization of the Ghetto," a man who, Zangwill notes, "had a latent feeling that Judaism had flourished before England was invented" (86). Though Hannah decides to escape on the *Seder* from his "cruel" religion with its "endless coil of laws" and make her own "exodus from slavery," she finally cannot leave.

The same theme appears in the story of Esther and Benjamin

Ansell and their father, Moses. Chapter 1 depicts little Esther's journey through "a dull, squalid, narrow thoroughfare in the East End of London" to a soup kitchen, described as a "cattle pen," where she will receive free soup and bread for her poverty-stricken family. The unrelieved poverty of the pious Moses Ansell's life, the precosity of Esther in school, and the strain of her "double life" as both Jew and Englishman leave her at the end of Book I brooding, still filled with "the beauties of Judaism" but also "looking forward hopefully to the larger life that the years would bring" (315). Esther's break from orthodoxy, which means one also with father, family, and tradition, does not come until Book II; but the break is imminent in Book I, where she reads the New Testament and wishes that she had "lived in the past, when Religion was happening" (175).

Her brother Benjamin, though shocked by her reading, has moved further than Esther from his father. Two chapters, "The Hope of the Family" (14) and "The Hope Extinct" (20) belong to Benjamin Ansell. Benjamin has been taken away from the Ansell family to an English boarding school; and, when we first meet him, he is returning for a visit to his family's Whitechapel garret, dressed and talking, Esther thinks, "like the pictures of little Lord Launceston in the Fourth Standard Reader" (168). Benjamin can no longer speak or understand "that beastly Yiddish," and he rejects Hebrew as "no good to anyone"; he confesses to Esther that he is ashamed of his father's shabby appearance and "those two beastly little curls at the side of his head" (171). Benjamin, who aspires to be a writer, anticipates his time of fame and fortune, when he can lift the family out of its poverty. But Benjamin becomes suddenly ill and dies. The separation of parent and child is stated most poignantly in Chapter 20, when Moses has come to his dying son's bedside. A nurse, observing that Moses cannot understand Benjy's English, nor Benjy Moses' Yiddish, says, "Isn't it a sad case? . . . They can't understand each other." But in Benjy's last delirious moments, he speaks Yiddish, "grown a child again." The father's "face lit up with joy. His eldest born had returned to intelligibility. There was hope still then. A sudden burst of sunshine flooded the room" (257). At the end, the father and son repeat together in Hebrew the *Shemah,* "the last declaration of the dying Israelite." "Both," Zangwill adds, "understood that."

Benjamin's story, then, parallels and underlines Hannah's, for both end with the reconciliation of child to father and with the affirmation of the values of Judaism. The title of the chapter depicting Benjy's death, "The Hope Extinct," is ironic; for, though the eldest son and hope of the family dies, he returns to Judaism at the last—and, as Moses thinks, "There was hope still then." So too the chapter depicting Hannah's decision not to flee from her father carries irony in its title, "Seder Night." On the night celebrating the exodus of her ancestors from slavery, Hannah plans to leave her father's house and his orthodoxy; but she is incapable of leaving that house, primarily because of the emotional power of the *Seder* ceremony itself. That theme of the return of the prodigal to the faith of his fathers serves to unify the separate stories in *Children of the Ghetto*.

Counterpointing the stories of Hannah and Benjy is the story of the Hyams and their children, told in Chapters 10 ("A Silent Family") and 17 ("The Hyams's Honeymoon"). Like Hannah, Esther, and Benjy, the Hyams' children are in rebellion against their parents: Daniel, because of the effect the Jewish Sabbath had on his ability to earn a living; Miriam, because she feels her position as schoolteacher places her socially above her parents' ghetto friends. Ironically, Daniel discovers that "when free thought waned . . ., although he never returned to his father's narrowness, he found the abhorred Sabbath sanctifying his life. It made a life a conscious voluntary sacrifice to an ideal, and the reward was a touch of consecration once a week" (125). But he, being "a silent man," never tells his parents this realization.

Daniel and Miriam are not reconciled to their parents, but the parents sacrifice themselves to the children and find an ample reward in their self-sacrifice. The Hyams resolve to go to America to free their children for advancement and marriage. In planning for this sacrifice (for they have no money and must face the hardship of starting anew in old age), they find love in what had always been a loveless marriage: "For fifteen years they had been drifting towards each other, . . . drifting nearer, near in silence, almost in unconsciousness. And now they had met. The supreme moment of their lives had come . . . love flooded their souls at last" (216). The struggle between the children of the ghetto and their parents is resolved in this story, then, by the parents, who, like the child in the Hannah-David plot, make a sacrifice for the sake of love.

The disparate stories in the book are unified not only by the themes of reconciliation and self-sacrifice but also by that of the search for a meaningful religion. This theme is introduced in the Proem, in which Zangwill laments the death of Judaea as "the vivid tints of the East [blur] into the uniform gray of English middle-class life" (xviii). The old men who "would have been . . . surprised . . . to be informed that they were orthodox" have disappeared, as have the color and vitality of ghetto life. The Proem ends with an *ubi sunt* lament recalling the "pathos sanctifying the joys that have been" (xix). The children of the ghetto— Hannah Jacobs, Esther and Benjamin Ansell, Miriam and Daniel Hyams, and others—have lost or are losing faith; and the grandchildren of the ghetto, in Book II, have not only lost faith but often deny their people, becoming, like Sir Asher Aaronsberg in Zangwill's short story "The Jewish Trinity," a combination of Jews, Englishmen, and anti-Semites.

Book II, *Grandchildren of the Ghetto,* begins with a fierce attack on Anglicized Jews, as the title of Chapter 1, "The Christmas Dinner," suggests. Early in this chapter Zangwill says that "the history of the Grandchildren of the Ghetto, which is mainly a history of the middle-classes, is mainly a history of isolation" (319). The scene of the dinner (actually, a Chanukah dinner) is the home of Mrs. Henry Goldsmith, an upper bourgeois Jewess; Mrs. Goldsmith's household remains kosher only because of the efforts of an old servant, Mary O'Reilly, a pious Catholic who served Henry Goldsmith's father and assumes that his children will be equally pious. Most of the Jews present at the dinner reject their Jewishness, though they observe some of the forms of Judaism. For example, they despise the idea of intermarriage but look on Yiddish as "vulgarity," often have Anglicized their names, and refuse to "spend Christmas" at Brighton because "so many Jews go there" (334–37).

The subject of conversation at the dinner is a book, *Mordecai Josephs,* which has scandalized West End Jews. Few details are given about the book, by an unknown writer, Edward Armitage, since those attacking it at the dinner insist they have not read it; but from what is said one can discern that the book is a Realistic portrayal of Jewry; it is, one guest says, by an author who "not only presents his characters but moralizes over them—actually cares whether they are good or bad, and has yearnings after the indefinable" (330). The West End Jews are horrified by the book because in it they are "badly treated"; apparently what they want from art depicting Jews is an apologia, not an analysis. In this scene Zangwill no doubt had in mind criticism of his own Realistic portrayal of Jewish life; his early story, "Motza Kleis," depicting market day in Jewry, had shocked his school administrators so much that they asked him never to publish another story without their permission. He probably also had in mind Amy Levy's *Reuben Sachs,* which had scandalized London Jews in 1888 because of its attempt at Realistic portrayal of London ghetto life.

It is no surprise to us when we later learn (Ch. 10) that Esther Ansell, one of the guests at the dinner, grown to intelligent womanhood under the patronage of Mrs. Goldsmith, is the author of *Mordecai Josephs.* Esther's search for a meaningful life when she has left the ghetto constitutes the major struggle in *Grandchildren of the Ghetto;* and, as in *Children of the Ghetto,* the conflict focuses on the emancipated versus the orthodox Jew. Esther claims that, because she has "lived among the brutal facts" of the ghetto, "the squalor and the misery" she endured there make her scorn "talk of the mission of Israel." In her former poverty she "yearned for a fuller, wider life, for larger knowledge"; and, since leaving the ghetto, she has had education and travel and "my fill of sunshine and beauty" (346–48). At Mrs. Goldsmith's party, Esther comes into direct conflict with young Raphael Leon, a highly intellectual orthodox Jew who laments the rejection of Judaism by Israel's great men, who discerns that Jews like Esther "are ignorant of our own ritual while admiring everything non-Jewish" (341), and who believes that the phrase "orthodox Jew" is a tautology. After she recovers from the shock of discovering an Oxford man who binds his phylacteries on his arm and forehead every morning, Esther accuses Raphael of having lived a sheltered life among his books; but she is nevertheless disturbed by him, especially when he tells her that he is editing a newspaper, *The Flag of Judah,* which will have as its purpose the conversion of Esther.

The conflict between father and child is continued in *Grandchildren of the Ghetto,* for Raphael replaces Moses Ansell in Esther's life. At the end of Chapter 2, Esther imagines Raphael and her father in "grotesque juxtaposition" (357-58); throughout half the novel, Esther struggles to find her place in Raphael's and the Goldsmith's world. She writes for *The Flag of Judah,* and she and Raphael and other intelligent young grandchildren of the ghetto debate questions of religion and art. Finally, however, Esther leaves both Raphael and the Goldsmiths and returns to the ghetto, writing to Raphael that his "narrow-minded [orthodox] friends . . . have cramped my soul. Now at last I am going to cut myself free" (456). Ironically, the cutting free means a return to White-chapel, "to her true home" and "to her father's primitive faith" (461), which she had in the past left with a sense of relief. Though she now feels herself an alien in the ghetto, she considers it her background, "a permanent sombre canvas" (466), and it is there that she begins to resolve the spiritual struggle that Raphael and his orthodoxy had started.

One of the reasons for Esther's break from the West End Jews is that she encounters an old ghetto friend, Levi Shemuel (Han-nah's brother), who now calls himself Leonard James and tells Esther, "I see you're like me; I never think of the Ghetto if I can help it" (425). Levi proposes marriage to Esther, and when she refuses him calls her "a *Schnorrer* [beggar] living on the charity of strangers," reminding her that she is the daughter of a peddler who "stood in the Lane with lemons and *schnorred* half-crowns of my father" (429–30). The violence of the scene with Levi turns her thoughts once more to the ghetto, especially to the *Seder* night long ago (depicted in the last chapter of *Children of the Ghetto*) "when she sat before the garret fire striving to picture the larger life of the future." That "larger life" outside the ghetto has proved unsatisfactory.

Just as Esther returns to the ghetto and all it represents— family and faith in the midst of unspeakable hardship—so does Levi return to his father; but not before a bitter break occurs. It is the *Seder* when Levi and Esther quarrel; and, as Esther is remembering that long-past *Seder* night, Levi is forgetting Esther with dinner at his club and entertainment at a music hall. Reb Shemuel, worried by his son's absence at the *Seder* table, goes to search for him and finds him leaving the theater with an actress: "For one awful instant, that seemed an eternity, the old man and the young faced each other across the chasm which divided their lives" (434). Levi decides to ignore his father; as he drives off, he tells the actress that Reb Shemuel is "only an old Jew who supplies me with cash" (435).

The break on this *Seder* between Levi and Reb Shemuel com-pletes the break that Hannah had not been able to make on the

*Seder* night when she was to elope with David Brandon (*Children of the Ghetto,* Ch. 25). But the Levi-Reb Shemuel story also parallels the Benjy-Moses Ansell story in *Children of the Ghetto.* Just as in his dying moments Benjy Ansell returns "to intelligibility" (Yiddish and Hebrew and his father's prayers), so too Levi eventually returns to his father. Hannah writes to Esther that Levi died "happy in the consciousness of father's forgiveness," uttering deathbed prayers with his father's phylacteries on his head and the *Talith* around him. The chapter of the reconciliation, entitled "The Prodigal Son," is the next-to-last chapter in *Grandchildren of the Ghetto;* and it serves as the final statement of the theme unifying both *Children of the Ghetto* and its sequel. Both children and grandchildren drift away from Judaism, but both return to it in moments of crisis.

As an adult, Esther witnesses in the West End Jewish community "the steady silent drift of the new generation away from the old landmarks"—toward reform, which "was cold, crude and devoid of magnetism" (439), or toward denial of Judaism. When she returns to the ghetto, she finds inspiration in Hannah Jacobs' example. Hannah's face shows, after ten years, a refinement and earnestness "almost spiritual, telling of suffering and patience, not unblent with peace" (485). After sacrificing herself to her father's law, Hannah has spent her life serving others in the ghetto; and Esther, meeting Hannah again, finds likewise a "sense of a mission—of a niche in the temple of human service which she had been predestined to fill" (488). She is able to see in the ghetto the misery and the failings, but she recognizes also the "illogical happiness" that flourishes there. Hannah Jacobs' story ends as Hannah persuades her father, by telling him of the sacrifice she made years before, to forgive Levi; when the father is reconciled to his prodigal son, Hannah feels that "My sacrifice was not in vain after all" (541).

Neither Hannah's sacrifice nor Esther's return is an intellectual commitment to Judaism. The emotional force of family and Jewish ritual made Hannah Jacobs stay in the ghetto, and the same force makes Esther return. And, just as Jewish holidays marked the progress of *Children of the Ghetto,* so too in *Grandchildren of the Ghetto* such holidays reflect Esther's growth. The latter book begins with "The Christmas Dinner" and ends with *Yom Kippur* (the Day of Atonement), after which Esther leaves for a new life in the New World. At the Goldsmiths, Esther finds no meaning in Jewish holidays. Chapter 6 begins with a statement of how Passover "brought no thrill to Esther now" (398). But, after her break with the Goldsmiths and after a period of service in the ghetto, Esther responds to the magnetism of the synagogue service on *Yom Kippur* (Ch. 18): "once again her dead self woke, her dead ancestors that would not be shaken off lived and moved in her." Filled with an "over-mastering impulse," she makes an affirmation of faith in a "half-hysterical" declaration; then she leaves for the New World, after having refused, at least for the moment, Raphael Leon's offer of marriage. Raphael has told her, "Somehow you seem to stand for Judaism. . . . I have come to conceive your life as an allegory of Judaism, the offspring of a great and tragic past with the germs of a rich blossoming, yet wasting with an inward canker" (535). If Esther is indeed a symbol of Judaism, her progress indicates that the fate of Judaism is to rise from the ghetto to prosperity and skepticism and then, dissatisfied with the new life, to return to the ghetto for direction.

In the closing chapters of *Grandchildren of the Ghetto,* the influence of Mrs. Humphrey Ward's *Robert Elsmere* is most evident. Even a character like Robert Elsmere—Joseph Strelitski— appears to accompany Esther to the New World. But perhaps a résumé of *Robert Elsmere* is first in order (since I suspect that *Robert Elsmere* is even less known to the modern reader than *Children of the Ghetto*—though both were immensely popular in their day). Robert Elsmere is an Anglican minister educated at Oxford; there the major influences on his life are a Pater-like tutor who rejects religion and social involvement and loves knowledge for its own sake, and a layman lecturer of religious temper who is skeptical of miracle. Elsmere marries a woman of rigid orthodoxy and saintly temperament, who is always struggling with Robert's tendencies to doubt. In his parish, Elsmere comes under the influence of the squire, a rationalist intellectual historian, whose conversation and writings cause Elsmere finally to break with the church—a break begun, however, much earlier, in his Oxford days.

The central struggle is Elsmere's attempt to find his way in the midst of conflicting religious forces—his loving but almost fanatically orthodox wife versus the rationalist and skeptical tutors and friends. Three attitudes toward religion are represented in the novel: the fundamentalist (Elsmere's wife), the atheist (Elsmere's

Oxford tutor and the squire), and the man groping for a meaning-ful religion (Elsmere and the Oxford layman lecturer). Elsmere breaks from orthodoxy and moves to London, where he begins his spiritual rehabilitation by social work among the poor. He has in the final book of the novel (entitled "Gain and Loss") started a new religion, "a new house of faith," "a new Company of Jesus," a Brotherhood among the workers. This religion is a compromise between the rationalist and enthusiast positions: it rejects miracle, but bases its philosophy on the humanity of Jesus. Thus the novel shows the collapse of orthodox Anglicanism among the intelligentsia of the nineteenth century, but it also insists that religious impulse has not died in the hearts of Elsmere and his working-class converts. Elsmere, however, makes only a beginning when, always sickly, he becomes ill and dies.

Both *Robert Elsmere* and *Children of the Ghetto* depict, then, the collapse of orthodoxy and the search for a meaningful religion to replace the old; neither book offers a final solution to the problem of faith in a skeptical world. Elsmere is beginning to work out a solution before he dies; Esther is making a beginning at the end of *Grandchildren of the Ghetto*. Joseph Strelitski, like Robert Elsmere, gives up his orthodox ministry as meaningless. Introduced in *Children of the Ghetto* as a young student at the Zionist meeting, Strelitski has become, in *Grandchildren of the Ghetto*, rabbi to the West End Jews; he is admired for his promise by all but Esther, who says that "He is eloquent, but his dogmatism irritates me. I don't believe he is sincere" (333).

Just as Elsmere gives up his parish in Surrey because he no longer accepts the forms and dogmas of Anglicanism, so Strelitski resigns his rabbinate, inspired by the example of Esther's flight from West End Jewry. He tells Raphael that "this damnable white tie has been choking the life and manhood out of me"—that he has become "the fief of a Rabbinate that is an anachronism, the bond-man of outworn forms, the slave of the *Shulcan Aruch* (a book the Rabbinate would not dare publish in English), the professional panegyrist of the rich" (509–10). He rejects ceremonial religion for "the brotherhood of man" (518). When Strelitski meets Esther again at the synagogue on the Day of Atonement, both have returned to the ghetto to begin the search for a purposeful life, just as Elsmere moves away from his country parish to the slums of London.

Zangwill's novel, however, ends more optimistically than Mrs. Humphrey Ward's. At the end of *Robert Elsmere,* the hero, the founder of the new religion, is dead; at the end of *Children of the Ghetto,* Esther and Strelitski are setting sail toward the New World. Zangwill's novel also ends more conservatively than Mrs. Humphrey Ward's. Whereas *Robert Elsmere* has as first step to a solution a permanent break with orthodoxy, *Grandchildren of the Ghetto* suggests that a step toward solution lies in acceptance of a common heritage: Strelitski tells Esther, "we are both Children of the Ghetto." Esther's parting words to Raphael are that Raphael's "allegory [of Esther as Judaism] seems turning in your favor, Raphael," a suggestion that a marriage between Raphael and Esther, or orthodox and emancipated, is possible, even probable. Whereas *Robert Elsmere* seems to suggest a solution in a new religion of brotherhood, which has its own service and its own ritual, *Children of the Ghetto* offers the possibility of a union of old and new, perhaps in an acceptance of the "common heritage" without the ceremonial forms. The orthodoxy rejected in *Grandchildren of the Ghetto* is that of the hypocritical West End Jews and the orthodoxy accepted is that of the struggling ghetto, where religion was not merely a form but a part of everyday life cementing the family of man.

## IV  The King of Schnorrers

Zangwill's best long work and perhaps the best of all his work is *The King of Schnorrers* (1894). First published in Jerome K. Jerome's *The Idler, The King of Schnorrers* is the only Zangwill novel readily available to the reading public; published by Dover in 1965, it has received more modern critical attention than any other of Zangwill's works. Bernard N. Schilling, in a Preface to the 1953 Shoe String Press edition, analyzes the humor of the novel, which he finds typical of Jewish humor—a self-directed humor providing relief from suffering and frustration.[14] Maurice Wohlgelernter in an introduction to the Dover edition likewise speaks of the book's "Jewish humor that cures folly with folly and like the comic spirit, makes game of 'serious' life."[15]

But it seems to me that the best way to understand the comic brilliance of *The King of Schnorrers* is not by regarding it exclusively as an example of Jewish humor but by placing it in its

English comic tradition. *The King of Schnorrers* is a comedy about a confidence man, in the tradition of Chaucer's "Canon's Yeoman's Tale" and of Ben Jonson's *Alchemist* or *Volpone*. The comedy in the novel depends not only on the incongruity between the beggar-hero's rags and his regal manner but also on his thwarting folly, not with folly, but by playing, Volpone-fashion, on the weaknesses and foibles of others.

The King of Schnorrers (Jewish beggars) is Manasseh Bueno Barzillai Azevedo da Costa; his name is made up of names of powerful, aristocratic, famous Jews,[16] and he himself is a member, though a lowly one, of the aristocratic Sephardic Jewish community. He is serious (he has no sense of humor); erudite, especially in Jewish law; precise, with an amazing eye for detail; and, above all, professional. He looks on schnorring as a profession, and spends much of the time coaching his future son-in-law in the fine art of schnorring. The plot of the novel shows Manasseh practicing that art, sometimes for personal profit, sometimes for the sheer pleasure of exercising his wit.

The short novel has only six chapters, and the work falls into three parts: in the first part (Chs. 1–2) we see Manasseh outwitting an individual; in the second part (Chs. 3–4) Manasseh and his fellow schnorrer, Yankelé, engage in a schnorring contest; and in the third part (Chs. 5–6) Manasseh outwits a group—the Sephardic *Mahamad* (ruling council) and the Sephardic synagogue. Manasseh's first victim is Joseph Grobstock, a rich member of the Ashkenazic community who is first seen passing out gifts of money in paper packets, arbitrarily giving some much and some little and amusing himself by watching the expressions of surprise among the beggars receiving his charity. Manasseh receives a paper packet which has nothing in it, and his outrage at the insult alarms Grobstock. Before the end of Chapter 1, Manasseh, by curses, insults, and snobbery (Manasseh is an aristocratic Sephardi), talks Grobstock out of the rest of his charity money, buys the fish Grobstock wants for dinner, obtains the right to Grobstock's cast-off clothes, and receives an invitation to Sabbath dinner.

The unfeeling and proud Grobstock is easy prey for the quick-witted Manasseh. Grobstock's snobbish alarm at the idea of having a ragged man to dinner makes him promise Manasseh his castoff clothes; we are hardly sorry for Grobstock, then, when Manasseh sells the clothes and comes to dinner, after all, in rags: we simply take delight in seeing the discomfiture of a snob. The title of Chapter 1—"Showing how the wicked philanthropist was turned into a fish porter"—suggests this comic humiliation of a rogue: the "wicked philanthropist" is punished at the end of Chapter 1 when Grobstock enters his own house behind Manasseh, carrying Manasseh's fish.

Chapter 2, "Showing how the king reigned," depicts the Sabbath dinner at Grobstock's, where Manasseh brings his friend Yankelé to "make the necessary third at grace." In spite of his dirt and rags, Manasseh flatters and impresses Mrs. Grobstock. At the end of this chapter we see Grobstock's pride deflated once more, as Manasseh magnanimously offers "to marry your daughter if you had one." Grobstock is shocked at the idea until he discovers that Manasseh means to act as a marriage broker:

"Oh, in *that* sense," said Grobstock, mollified in one direction, irritated in another.

"In what other sense? You do not think I, a Sephardi, would marry her myself!"[17]

Thus the King of Schnorrers snubs Grobstock, reducing him to the level of subject of the king.

The major complication of the novel is Yankelé's desire to marry Manasseh's beautiful daughter; Yankelé is a Tedesco, and Manasseh at first considers the request an insult: "A Sephardi cannot marry a Tedesco! It would be a degradation" (54). But Yankelé is an equal to Manasseh in wit and a worthy crown prince for the King of Schnorrers. Yankelé has to demonstrate his worth by schnorring a dinner from the Rabbi Remorse Red-Herring, described as "the meanest of mankind" (82). Chapters 3 and 4 show Yankelé and Manasseh at their best, engaging in wit contests with each other, schnorring their way to a box seat at the theater and later to a dinner with the stingiest man in the ghetto. At the end of Chapter 4, Yankelé has passed the test and won Manasseh's daughter, the fair Deborah.

Wohlgelernter regards Manasseh's statement that "A Sephardi cannot marry a Tedesco!" as evidence of a fault in Manasseh "far worse" than the other absurdities satirized in the book;[18] but to see Manasseh as a prejudiced snob is to misread his character. Though Manasseh proudly and frequently refers to his Sephardic lineage, he does it primarily to embarrass and bully worse snobs, such as Grobstock. Manasseh treats Yankelé, on the other hand, as a friend. Significantly, it is Yankelé that Manasseh brings to Grobstock's dinner in Chapter 2; and, though Manasseh does not want to consent to the marriage, Yankelé's persistence and his wit finally win Manasseh's consent. At the beginning of Chapter 4, after Yankelé has just offered an intricate argument for the marriage, we are told, "Manasseh Bueno Barzillai Azevedo da Costa was so impressed by his would-be son-in-law's last argument that he perpended it in silence for a full minute. When he replied, his tone showed even more respect than had been infused into it by the statement of the aspirant's income. Manasseh was not of those to whom money is a fetish; he regarded it merely as something to be had for the asking. It was intellect for which he reserved his admiration. That was strictly not transferable" (78). Manasseh's values are based, therefore, not on wealth or family but on intellectual agility. After Yankelé impresses Manasseh with his intellect, Manasseh sets the task; at this point the two are merely playing— schnorring for schnorring's sake. The game even has rather elaborate rules; Manasseh later criticizes Yankelé's conning the rabbi by exaggeration and lying for, according to Manasseh, Yankelé's exaggerations were an unnecessary "waste of good material," and "A first-class *Schnorrer* never lies" (100).

The final chapters show Manasseh talking the Sephardim into accepting Yankelé into the Sephardic community. The *Mahamad* echoes Manasseh's original objection to the marriage: "Do you not know that the union you contemplate is disgraceful and degrading to you, to your daughter, and to the community which has done so much for you? What! A Sephardi marry a Tedesco! Shameful" (116). But Manasseh triumphs, as he exercises all his intellectual and persuasive powers in haughty insult, in bids for sympathy, in condescending forgiveness of slights, in verbal quibbles, in citation of the law, in a social defense of schnorring, in accusations of prejudice, and in threats. With final inspired audacity, he accuses the *Mahamad* of prejudice against the poor, asserts that the Ashkenazic community "waxes daily in wealth and greatness while you sleep in your sloth," and then plops down in the president's chair. The president, who has rushed to the bell to call for help, has an attack of apoplexy; Manasseh, who orders water for him, takes command of the council. Manasseh then moralizes on the *de casibus* theme and leaves the assembly "cowed," wavering "before his words, like reeds before the wind, or conscience-stricken kings before fearless prophets" (127).

The final chapter shows Manasseh at his most kingly; Yankelé has been "called to the Reading of the Law like a true-born Portuguese" (128), and Manasseh pledges, in a dramatic display of beneficence, one hundred pounds to the synagogue. He then collects the money by schnorring: appealing to the sick president's superstition, to the pride of other vain Sephardim, to the vanity of a fop, to the sense of duty of his cousin Barzillai, and once more to Grobstock's snobbery. When Manasseh finally gives the money to the synagogue, it has, because of Grobstock's investment of it, become six hundred pounds. With the unpledged five hundred, Manasseh sets up a Da Costa Fund "for a poor and deserving member of the congregation" and then appoints himself recipient of it.[19]

The theme of the novel is not, as Wohlgelernter says, "disunity among Jews in the face of adversity,"[20] but the comic discomfiture of fools and knaves. Like Ben Jonson's Subtle or Volpone, Manasseh is the intellectual superior of the people he cheats. But Manasseh lacks the criminality of Jonson's Alchemist; Manasseh always operates within the law; indeed, he does not even approve of telling lies to get money. He is—as the title of the book says— regal. Early in the novel, Grobstock, impressed by Manasseh's ability to command him and his servant, asks himself, "Did not a natural aristocracy ooze from every pore of his mysterious visitor? Was not every tone, every gesture, that of a man born to rule?" (41) At the theater, Manasseh commands a box seat and, by an accidental confusion of the bored audience, receives an ovation as he sits down. Before the *Mahamad,* Manasseh takes control; at the end, sitting on the president's throne, he is issuing orders and moralizing. At the synagogue, "he dignified his shabby vestments, stuffing them with royal manhood, and wearing his snuff-colored over-garment like a purple robe" (128–29).

Manasseh is able to rule because he finds himself in a kingdom of fools and knaves. The world cheated by Manasseh is worse than he—worse intellectually and morally. In addition to the snobbish Grobstock are the cockney doorkeeper to the theater, who is impressed by an imperious manner and a name; the mean and greedy Rabbi Remorse Red-Herring; the *Mahamad,* which,

Zangwill says, is an "oligarchy [which] would undoubtedly be a byword for all that is arbitrary and inquisitorial but for the widespread ignorance of its existence" (105). The final chapter shows a variety of foolish people: the superstitious president of the *Mahamad;* Rodrigues, who admits that he would give money to a man in a carriage but not to a schnorrer; a fop; and other proud Sephardi, who contribute money for fear of appearing mean before the new member.

Of all the characters in the book, only Yankelé is worthy of Manasseh's respect—so worthy that Manasseh accepts him as son-in-law and sees that Yankelé is admitted to the Sephardic synagogue. In the comedy, Yankelé functions as witty servant; like Face in *The Alchemist* or Mosca in *Volpone,* he lends a comic spirit to the serious con game his master plays. Manasseh's game, like Subtle's and Volpone's, is ostensibly for personal gratification; but Zangwill's comic presentation of that game, like Jonson's, comments on a world so foolish that it is fair game for a con man who, by cheating it, exposes it to ridicule.

## V  The Master

Zangwill's next novel, *The Master* (1895), departs from the comic and also from Jewish subject matter. A long novel, it traces an artist's life from boyhood to artistic maturity in late middle age, and it contains tedious sections; nevertheless, it is a notable contribution to late nineteenth-century Realistic literature depicting the artist as a young man. In this novel Zangwill seems to be following the advice of George Gissing's realist in *New Grub Street* (1891), who wishes to show "the fateful power of trivial incidents." Part of the tedium of *The Master* arises from Zangwill's conviction that life is an accumulation of tedious, exhausting events which assume significance only if an artist shows their purpose and poetry. A man's character, Zangwill believes, is made up of trivial events: "The long, endless years, crowded with petty episodes and uniformities, and moving like a cumbrous, creeping train that stops at every station . . . color the fabric of our future lives, eating into our souls like a slow acid." [21] In the novel, we see the "episodes and uniformities" that create a master painter, Matthew Stang. Like Gissing's *New Grub Street* and other artist stories at the end of the century, *The*

*Master* explores the artist's life in London, where an artistically ignorant public allows talent to starve and artistic glibness to prosper. Matthew Stang, like the artist-hero in Gissing or James, finds neglect and poverty the result of earnest work and genuine talent; he also finds that marriage for an artist is an almost fatal mistake.

*The Master* is divided into three books, the first dealing with Matt's youth in Nova Scotia, the second with his failure in London and return to Nova Scotia, and the third with his cheap success in a London which lionizes him once he begins painting to please the public. Each book shows a gradual fall, ending with a partial recovery. Book I, set in Acadia, is a pessimistic vision of the simple, primitive life. It shows Matt's early disillusionment with his fellow man, his increasing skepticism, and his patient work toward an ideal of studying art in London, where a famous uncle, also an artist and also named Matthew Stang, has made a fortune. Chapter 1, "Solitude," depicts a Stang family scene: Matt and his crippled brother Billy overhear a violent argument between their mother and sister; the irrational, emotionally unstable mother threatens suicide and is stopped from leaving the house only by the arrival of a letter saying that Matt's sailor father has been drowned at sea. This melodramatic chapter introduces the major influences on Matt's character: the unhappy, morbid mother, who is always threatening "to throw up her position" as housewife and mother, and the dead father, whose face haunts the child and man. After years of apprenticeship in Cobequid Village, Matt finally goes to Halifax and a larger life. The final chapters of Book I depict Matt's work in a furniture store in Halifax, his abortive attempt to go to the United States, his first experience of poverty in a strange city, and his gradual accumulation of money for London. The last chapter, "Exodus," suggests an end to his bondage; but his departure for London is saddened by a visit with his mother, who has finally become dangerously ill and who has been committed to an asylum in Halifax.

Just as Book I began with a disillusioning introduction to the simple, happy rustic life, Book II opens with a description of the ugliness of London, which in Matt's childhood was a symbol of the beautiful and grand. In Chapter 1 Matt meets his Uncle Matt, who had represented the successful artist; the uncle, he finds, has failed to make a name in art but has succeeded in making a fortune by buying and selling others' art. Matt begins to study art under a second-rate painter, and through his wealthy cousin, Herbert Stang, he meets and talks with the avant-garde artists of the day. The friendship with Herbert, however, causes Matt's collapse in London. Herbert, also an artist, is given an abundant allowance by his father; but Matt's own small savings dwindle as he and Herbert explore artistic London. Herbert is of no help when Matt is finally out of money. Matt tries numerous jobs to save himself from ruin: he draws for magazines and papers; he even tries factory work; then he becomes a bird stuffer for a taxidermist.

During Matt's period of decline, Herbert wins a Gold Medal for young artists from the Royal Academy. The painting submitted, on a biblical subject, is one which he and Matt had worked on together; in fact, Matt had painted most of it. Inspired by Herbert's example, Matt, while he is a bird stuffer, paints "The Paradise of Birds," which he submits to the Royal Academy. It is rejected, and Matt, discouraged and physically ill, returns home in defeat.

His suffering in London has caused in Matt a shift in values. He now desires money over art. In Nova Scotia, he makes money as a painter of carriages, houses, signs, and ship figureheads; but as in all his other efforts, he suffers an unexpected' reversal of fortune when a shipbuilder for whom he is working goes bankrupt. Matt suddenly finds himself in debt and, shortly afterward, in debtor's prison. When he is released, he is easily persuaded to marry the daughter of a friendly old merchant in exchange for her dowry and annual income. Book II ends with Matt's approaching marriage to Rosina Coble.

Book III opens with a flat statement of the misery of Matt's marriage to a woman of no intellectual or esthetic sensitivity. He has another painting rejected by the Royal Academy; and, in desperation, he studies the popular paintings in the Academy and in the Grosvenor galleries and cynically paints a sentimental painting called "Motherhood," which, accepted by the Academy, brings him fame. The rest of Book III shows Matt a social and financial success. He has alienated himself from his wife and children and falls in love with an intellectual, cultivated lady, Eleanor Wyndwood. He resumes his old friendship with Herbert

Stang, and he and Herbert woo Eleanor and her young, cynical companion, Olive Regan. Finally, Matt, completely estranged from his wife, wins Eleanor's love, only to decide that he must sacrifice his love and his art for the sake of his moral obligation to his wife and family. The end of the book has him back with his wife in a monotonous, essentially unhappy life. He discovers, however, that the move home has not wrecked his art; in fact, he has finally begun his real work as artist, having renounced fame, riches, and love and become "master of his soul at last" (517).

The characteristic Zangwillian theme of self-sacrifice for the sake of others is given no dramatic treatment in this novel. Matt writes Eleanor a farewell letter and returns home to find his wife at church and his brother Billy and son Davie filled with complaints: "Thus tamely passed off the great renunciation scene— the crisis of his life—like everything else in his life, unlike what he had imagined beforehand" (515). The sacrifice is not, however, in vain. Book III ends as the other two books ended—with the promise of a better life. But, at the end of Book III, instead of placing his faith in escape to London, as at the end of Book I, or in money, as at the end of Book II, Matt has now accepted mundane reality—specifically, his prosaic wife and family. And he finds in this ordinary life the inspiration for his painting: "he longs to paint the beauty that lies unseen of grosser eyes, the poetry of mean streets and every-day figures, to enrich and hallow life by revealing some sweep of a great principle that purifies and atones" (522). Zangwill's artist comes to recognize— as Zangwill himself does in all his work—not only "the fateful power of trivial incidents" but also the beauty and moral significance of such incidents.

The central conflict in the novel begins when, in Cobequid Village, Matt is cursed by Mad Peggy, who predicts that he will "thirst and thirst and thirst for everything, and never be satisfied, never . . . have anything you want" (67). Throughout most of the book, Matt impatiently pursues an ideal: at first he believes it to be London and his Uncle Matthew; then he believes it is financial success; and finally, the beautiful Eleanor Wyndwood. All prove disappointing—London is ugly, and his uncle is no artist; fame and riches leave him dissatisfied; and Eleanor refuses to sacrifice reputation for honesty. Matt's attempt to escape an ordinary life is like his mad mother's; she had once pleaded with him to take her away, "where we can be happy and free," away from "all this humdrum life" (130).

As Matt suffers defeat after defeat, he also echoes his mother's hysterical threat "to throw up the position"; in Book III he does indeed "throw up the position" of husband and father, moving into a studio away from his family. Later, when Eleanor is leaving for Paris and he has not found strength to tell her of his love, he, like his mother before him, contemplates suicide, and the word choice echoes his mother: "The position was hopeless; were it not best to throw it up?" (471)

Matt is finally recalled to a moral life and to art by a visit to a childhood sweetheart, Ruth Hailey, now a middle-aged spinster working for the Feminist cause. Matt meets Ruth in Paris, and she tells him of "the tragic pettiness of the life-struggle for single girls—the stifled aspirations, the abortive longings, the tears in the night" (491). She hints of her own past trials, saying that from them she has learned sympathy and service; without them, she says, "My life might have been wasted in mere happiness." Her acceptance of unfulfilled ideals gives Matt the strength to renounce his newly won love of Eleanor and to stop his search for "mere happiness," as Ruth has done: "There did not seem to be enough happiness to go round. Who was he, to be selected for a special helping? Who was he more than his mate the scavenger, more than any other of the human souls he had met in his diversified career, more than his fellow-lodgers in the slums of Holborn or Halifax, or his fellow-passengers on board *The Enterprise*, or the blind woman who caned chairs in the basement of the house of the Rotherhithe bird-stuffer? Why should he be happy?" (508) The renunciation becomes, ironically, the source of artistic inspiration: "What he had wanted he had not got; by the time he had got it he had not wanted it; whatever he had set out to do he had not done, and whatever he had done he had not foreseen. And out of all this travail of the soul was born his Art—strong, austere, simple" (517).

Throughout the novel Matt struggles to mature as an artist, and the development of his art reflects the development of his character. His early art is untutored, honest, and exuberant; he draws scenes from nature on pieces of bark, in the snow, in his schoolbooks and the family Bible. As soon as he leaves Cobequid

Village, he learns, however, that salable art is often prostituted art; he literally peddles his talent, traveling about painting signs and portraits, to earn money to go to London. In London, he studies earnestly at an art class but is forced by poverty to become a hack: "It was not a happy time for Matt, this period of spiritless work by day and spiritless study by night, his soul chafing alike against the degradations of life and the routine of school" (233).

In self-disgust he resolves to give up art: "Rather an honest artisan than a dishonest artist" (236). But the working man's dreary, monotonous life sends him back to art—this time the art of bird-stuffing. This job is one of his worst; the atmosphere is infected with poisonous fumes and the art is fraud: "He not only stuffed the skins . . . , but arranged baskets of wax-fruit . . . and paper flowers and cases of shells with moss and sea-weeds and pyramids of pebbles. And he made mock red coral out of balls of brown paper, dipped into a hot composition of beeswax and rosin, and stuck it on wooden stands with many-hued shells variegating it, and preserved insects creeping prettily over it; likewise he manufactured wax-flowers to replace break-ages; hollow frauds" (266-67).

During this time, he paints "The Paradise of Birds," a picture "uncompromisingly imaginative," depicting freed birds in a gorgeous wood around "a divine female figure" and "a beautiful boy playing upon an oaten pipe" at her feet. The Royal Academy's rejection of this painting sends him home to Nova Scotia. Though there he aims only at earning money, he incidentally transforms a village with his painting of signboards, houses, carriages, and store blinds. By such mundane painting, he throws "a glamour over life" in the little village, touching "the sleeping souls of his fellows to livelier issues, though his own interest in Art was numb" (276–77). This worthy work is soon over, however, and his next work lands him in prison.

This experience, followed by his unhappy marriage, makes him abhor life and sends him searching more avidly for "that timeless realm wherein ideal beauty dwells." He rejects real life: "Real life was Deacon Hailey and his mad mother and Billy and Rosina and his uncle and the grimy denizens of the London slums and the blackguardly crowd at the Fleet Street public-house and the lewd workmen in the Starsborough ship-yard. But

Art was . . . that imaginary world which man's soul had called into being to redress the balance of the Real" (311). In this mood, he paints for the Royal Academy a painting illustrating lines from Matthew Arnold's "The Forsaken Merman"; the picture showed "a woman, with a soul, throned amid a lower race, yet yearning for the higher spiritual fervors." [22] This painting, like "The Paradise of Birds," is also rejected; in despair, Matt gives up and paints "Motherhood" and a biblical painting, both of which are accepted by the Royal Academy. The years of his fame bring him commissions and adulation, but he is "always postponing the time when he would start upon the real artistic work of his life" (321); he paints portraits and works such as "Ideal Womanhood," which Herbert says is rather "Ideal moonshine."

When Matt falls in love with Eleanor Wyndwood, he begins to feel that, under her influence, he could paint the ideal. What he does not realize is that, under her influence, he can paint nothing at all. In all the time that he is courting Eleanor, he paints only a portrait of her, and that is for Herbert, who is painting Eleanor in order to be near her friend Olive. When Matt cannot declare his love, he begins a painting illustrating a Dante Gabriel Rossetti sonnet, "Love's Fatality"; but he destroys this painting. Then follow weeks "without any definite product. He was searching, but he could not find" (467).

He does not begin painting again until he, in defeat once more, returns to his wife, Rosina. To his surprise, "in this homely environment to which his soul was native," he can "produce faithfully and finely the work it was in him to do" (517). Here he paints "The Pain of the World," showing the figure of his mother as he had last seen her; "The Persecutors," drawing on a memory of his crippled brother's degradation at the hands of tormenting children; and "A Woman," combining Ruth Hailey and Eleanor Wyndwood against the background of a Paris sunrise. In contrast to his past yearning for the ideal, "to-day he yearns to paint the poetry of the Real. . . . He needed no woman's inspiration, nor the stimulus of cultured cliques. Alone he faces the realities of life and death without intervening veils of charming illusion, no longer craving to filter the honest sunlight through stained cathedral windows or to tarnish the simplicity of the grave with monumental angels" (521).

He becomes master of his art when he becomes master of his life. Two kinds of mastery are represented in the novel—that of Herbert, and that of Matt. Herbert's desire is a carefree, joyous life; he is assisted in this objective by his father's wealth, by his untroubled ability to postpone debts and exploit his friends, and by his well-bred manner and easygoing nature; at the end of the novel he is engaged to the woman he loves, Olive Regan, and life promises him more happiness. At one point, Matt views Herbert as "the real Master—the Master of life" (338). Matt, on the other hand, represents a mastery of self through rejection of personal happiness. He is recognized as a master in art before he deserves the title; he is called "my Master—now and ever" by Eleanor Wyndwood (478). But Ruth Hailey speaks of another as her master: she says that she is grateful for her sufferings, for "else I should never have learned to sympathize as I do, and I should not have served the Master" (492). The final chapter, entitled "The Master," shows a Matt Stang now "master of his soul," and consequently true master of his art. The final words in the novel have spiritual import, partially echoing Ruth's Christianity, as Matt "asks himself what Master he has followed in his sacrifice, or what Master, working imperturbably, moulds human life at his ironic, inscrutable will" (523).

## VI The Mantle of Elijah

After *The Master*, Zangwill's next novel, *The Mantle of Elijah* (1900), is a disappointment. Though its theme, the corruption of modern politics, was one about which Zangwill felt strongly, his treatment of it in *The Mantle of Elijah* resulted in the least effective of all his novels. The novel lacks adequate character and plot development; it lectures when it should dramatize; and the world view expressed in it lacks coherence. In this novel Zangwill seems to be groping for values; the book seems hastily thought through and just as hastily put together. Strangely, the abundant detail that critics object to in his other novels is needed in this one. We are left uninterested in the leading characters and unconvinced that they have solved any problems.

The central figure in the novel is Allegra Marshmont, the daughter of a British cabinet minister; she is one of those women one finds frequently in late nineteenth-century fiction: a young woman who, like a George Eliot, Henry James, or Thomas Hardy heroine, wants to make something of her life. Chapter 1 shows her toiling over a long poem in heroic couplets about fame, a poem which she abandons shortly afterward when her father shatters her illusions about the glory of war. She gives up her childish literary endeavor for a passion for politics and for a desire "to sink one's self, to serve, to minister, to be caught up into the splendor of a great life!"[23] She goes to work for her father, who introduces her to a young Radical political aspirant, Bob Broser. Sensing greatness in Broser, Allegra marries him, only to find him compromising his Radical principles on his way to political greatness. She is saved from the despair brought on by her husband's moral failure by a poet, Raphael Dominick, a detached, gentle man espousing the Nietzschean *übermensch* philosophy and hoping for the evolution of a better mankind. At the end of the novel Allegra, having witnessed her husband's spectacular rise to the premiership, is leaving her husband to begin a new life.

The political satire in the novel focuses on the unscrupulous Broser, who begins his career supporting the pacifist and social reform ideals of Allegra's father and rises to power by supporting an imperialistic war. The antiwar sentiments of the novel, which was written during the Boer War, are expressed by Allegra's father, the Elijah of the title, who wrecks his career rather than sanction a war. In the first of the two books of the novel, war with the backward nation of Novabarba is the cause of a public and private disaster for Allegra's father. He resigns his ministry when war is declared, and he loses his oldest son in the war. Allegra gets her first insight into war fever when an angry mob attacks her father and throws rocks at his house during the Novabarbese war; at that time, she and Broser, her father's assistant, pledge to "make an end of war" (191). In Book II, England once more goes to war with Novabarba, this time with Broser's approval. He explains to Allegra, "If I add Novabarba to the Empire, I shall ultimately become Premier" (306); he justifies the war by using the argument of "the white man's burden," but Allegra says he wades to power through blood (307). She had hoped that Broser would wear the mantle of her pacifist father.

The allusion to Elijah's mantle is explained by Raphael Dominick, who tells Allegra that the Jews expect a Messiah "after Elijah reappears." To Allegra's question, "And what is Elijah to do?" Raphael answers, "To bring peace into the world" (392). According to the novel, the Messiah has not yet appeared; but it is time for his appearance. Broser made a mockery of Elijah's pacifism, but Raphael Dominick may prove more worthy of the mantle. Raphael first appears in Book II, after Allegra has been praying for a deliverer from her despair. Allegra sees Raphael throughout as the means of her salvation: she first recognizes in him "the face . . . of a modern priest who could understand the modern soul"; after she tells him her troubles, she looks to him for guidance, saying, "I could follow you . . . like the women who followed Christ" (270, 290). Raphael, like Allegra, is without religion; he says that the only way he could bear the world was to become a detached spectator of scenes of human misery. But he falls in love with Allegra, and his love saves him from his death-in-life, just as he saves Allegra from her dead life with Broser.

One of the major weaknesses of the novel is that Raphael Dominick, dead to the world, never comes alive as a character either. He comes into the novel a mysterious, disillusioned, retiring person; all we know of him comes through exposition of his poverty-stricken, unhappy childhood or through his analysis of humankind in comments not unlike those made by other sympathetic characters in the novel. As a result, when he declares his love for Allegra (Bk. II, Ch. 20), we are unprepared to believe his change from detachment to involvement.

The novel also suffers from the omission of incident. In *The Master,* Zangwill focuses on a few characters for over five hundred pages of small print; in *The Mantle of Elijah,* he attempts to trace the lives of a profusion of characters in a book about half the size. The crucial years during which Allegra loses respect for her husband are not presented: Book I ends with the betrothal; Book II begins nine years later with Allegra sorrowful and disillusioned. Before the end of Book I, we know that Broser is conniving and ruthless, so that we are not surprised that Allegra has been unhappy with him; but we need more preparation for Allegra's utter devastation of soul in the first chapter of Book II. Book I introduces a set of potentially interesting characters—Allegra; her father; his imperious, unreasonable Welsh wife; his witty, affectionate Radical friend, William Fitzwinter; Allegra's aunt, the duchess of Dalesbury, one of those magnificent semicomic Victorian dowagers who makes the world conform to her view of it; Bob Broser, a young politician ready to sacrifice a sick wife to his personal triumph. Book I also provides background for a book about these people whose lives have touched each other. But then in Book II we find that Zangwill has skipped that book, and we are in a new setting (Italy) years later; we meet new characters— Raphael and his friend, Margaret Engelborne—whose stories make up sixteen of the twenty-five chapters of Book II.

Apart from these structural flaws, the novel raises questions about its final statement. The satire against Broser is clear, but what is the alternative to the Brosers of the world? One alternative is the intelligent woman, who, freed of her desire to submerge herself in another's character, turns her back on such as Broser to seek a better future. Another is the philosophical man, vitalized by love. Another alternative is the principled statesman, like Allegra's father. Also opposed to Broser are people like Allegra's sister Joan, whose life is devoted to caring for suffering people and who at the end of the novel is returning from a trip to war-torn Novabarba to work for the Feminist cause, because "The men have failed to produce civilization" (438). Another alternative would even seem to be the old duchess of Dalesbury, who, in spite of her Tory views and snobbery, is affectionate and motherly to Allegra; significantly, Allegra turns to the duchess when she plans to make her flight at the end of the novel. Finally, opposed to Broser is the long-suffering Margaret Engelborne, who is described by Raphael as the "only Christian" he knows (303); Margaret is a motherly, mystical, creative, totally selfless, pious girl who allows her health to deteriorate in her devotion to a dying sister.[24] Obviously, we have in the novel an array of alternatives to Broser and the war he encourages, but we are left with questions about which one (or ones) we are to accept. The final statement may be that each moral individual finds his own alternative to Broser's way, but that statement is also not clear in the novel.

This is not to deny that some merit exists in the novel. There is some potent political satire, especially on Jingoistic patriotism and on the "Will Success Spoil Bob Broser?" theme. There are some excellent bon mots: "Politics is only inconsistency reduced

to a career" (353); "Only the little criminals are put in prison.
The big are put in the Cabinet" (388). And, finally, there are
some interesting characters whose story, alas, is never told.

## VII    Jinny the Carrier

*The Mantle of Elijah* was the last novel Zangwill wrote for many
years. After the turn of the century Zangwill turned his attention
to political and social questions and his creative energies to the
drama. His last novel, *Jinny the Carrier,* published in 1919, is
based on his three-act play of the same name, produced in Boston
in 1905. This last novel, though not without faults, shows an
ability to capture atmosphere and to create character that makes
us regret the years that Zangwill wrote drama instead of novels.
As it stands, *Jinny the Carrier* is an anachronism, showing no evidence of having been written in the twentieth century. Set in rural
England in the middle of the nineteenth century, the novel, in its
reversion to a literary art reflecting that leisurely, slow-paced life,
recaptures the life of that day. Zangwill's Epistle Dedicatory,
addressed to his "dear Aunt by adoption," says that he has written
a "bland" novel, "one to be read when in bed with a sore throat." [25]
And *Jinny the Carrier* is a remarkable example of that genre—
remarkable because of its deliberate exclusion of any hint of the
twentieth century with its Great War, its alienated youth, and its
avant-garde art.

On an "elaborate canvas," with "slowness and minuteness of . . .
method," Zangwill attempts "to seize the essence of Essex" in an
admittedly romantic tale. Zangwill also describes the "bland"
novel: "Such a novel must, I conceive, begin with 'once upon a
time' and end with 'they all lived happy ever after,' so that my
task is simply to fill in the lacuna between these two points, and
supply the early-Victorian mottoes, while even the material was
marked out for me by Dr. Johnson's definition of a novel as 'a
story mainly about love' " (v–vii). The novel does indeed begin
"Once upon a time," and it ends with Jinny's belief that they will
"all live—wherever they all lived—happy ever after." In between
these points are over six hundred pages devoted partially to the
love story of Jinny and Will Flynt but primarily to a re-creation
of the Essex countryside and its inhabitants in a more idyllic day.
The first half of the book places Jinny, the rural carrier for Chip-

stone and environs, and Will, the adventurous young man returned from America, in their milieu. That milieu is one of placid and unthinking acceptance of life, enlivened only by religious bicker-ings among the narrowly fundamentalist sects of Jinny's village.

The first chapter, "Bundock on His Beat," introduces the simple rural folk, as the mail carrier, Bundock, delivers a letter to Frog Farm, the home of Caleb and Martha Flynt. The fact that this letter causes a kind of crisis in the Flynt household suggests the level of suspense that the novel maintains; and the interminable debate of Caleb and Martha about someone suitable to read the letter (neither of them can read) and their anxious speculations about its contents suggest the pace the rest of the novel follows. Chapters 2 and 3, "Jinny on Her Rounds" and "Jinny at Her Homes," introduce the heroine, an orphan who took over her grandfather's carrying business when the old man became too old to continue. We are assured that she is no heroine of poetry: "She certainly did not dress the part, for despite the witchery of the bonnet, her workaday skirt and stout shoes proclaimed the village girl, as her hands proclaimed the drudge who scoured and scrubbed and baked and dug and manured: indeed what with her own goats, and her farmyard commissions, she was almost as familiar with the grosser aspects of animal life as that strangely romanti-cized modern figure, the hospital nurse" (39–40). Into Jinny's life comes her childhood sweetheart, Will Flynt, returned to his home from America with just enough money to start him "on his way" (Ch. 4).

The central conflict in the novel is between the lovers: Will objects to Jinny's carrying, which he considers an unwomanly occupation; and Jinny objects to Will's objections. No one else in Chipstone objects to Jinny's work, not because Chipstone embraces Feminist ideas but because Jinny is a part of the routine of their lives. From her childhood, Jinny had made the rounds with her grandfather in his old horse-drawn cart, and she gradually began driving alone as her grandfather aged. Will was absent during the transition, and he is shocked: "A respectable girl like that—why, what was the world coming to? Sent gadding about the country like a trollop, perched up horsily behind a carter's whip—this was what little Jinny had been allowed to grow up into" (135). When Jinny and Will first meet after years of separa-tion, they argue about her work; and she irritates him by refusing to be shocked at his reference to "Bloomerites" (Feminists) in

America and by asserting—once she is challenged—her own
Feminist ideas. From this point the two engage in a battle of the
sexes in which a series of debates brings them, finally, into each
other's arms.

The novel's structure, after the opening expository and descrip-
tive chapters, is built around the duels. When Will objects to her
summoning people to the cart with blasts on her coach horn, the
argument leads to Jinny's challenging Will to a contest playing
the coach horn. The horn-blowing competition ends with the two
spending an idyllic afternoon in the woods together (Ch. 7,
"Comedy of Corydon and Amaryllis"), an afternoon spoiled, however, by another argument, this time about Jinny's commission to
buy a horse at the cattle fair. Will argues that a woman has no
business at the fair; and, to prevent Jinny from fulfilling her un-
ladylike commission, Will bids against her and purchases the only
two suitable horses ("Cupid and Cattle," Ch. 8). This apparent
triumph almost turns to defeat for Will when he learns that the
man commissioning Jinny to buy has changed his mind.

But the purchase of the horses leads to the major, and final,
duel: Will buys a coach and goes into the carrying business in
competition with Jinny. In "Two of a Trade" (Ch. 9) Will begins
to take Jinny's customers with his flashy coach, "The Flynt Flyer,"
and speedy horses. Chapters 10–11 depict Jinny's failure in business; "Winter's Tale," Chapter 11, is the low point in Jinny's
fortunes, with her increasing poverty and alienation from Will.
The turning point is a flood—a February thaw that covers Frog
Farm, drowns Will's horses, and destroys the coach. Because
Jinny's old horse and cart are unharmed, she rescues the Flynts
and regains her old customers. And she and Will finally give up
their dueling and admit that love has motivated the rivalry from
the beginning.

In the final chapter, as we might expect from its title, "The
Course of True Love," their love does not run smoothly. Will and
Jinny's grandfather in an earlier argument have taken foolish
oaths: the grandfather by saying that Will cannot enter his house
except on his hands and knees; Will by replying that he will not
enter unless the grandfather carries him in; but both men obsti-
nately refuse to break their oaths. Furthermore, Will has no money
and no prospects and decides that he must emigrate to Australia
to find land or gold; and Jinny cannot go with him because there
is no one to care for her old grandfather.

The problems are resolved by farcical-melodramatic-comic means. Will by an accident is carried into Jinny's house (on his hands and knees) in a trunk, in a farcical scene reflecting, Zangwill says, "The very soul of old English mirth" (580). The more serious problems are solved by the melodramatic revelation of a cache of money belonging to an old shepherd befriended by Jinny; with this money, her grandfather elopes with an old (a very old) sweetheart, who has just been committed to the county poorhouse. The novel ends with three marriages: one of Jinny's old suitors marries one of Will's old girlfriends, Jinny's grandfather elopes with his old sweetheart, and Jinny and Will are now free to marry and "live . . . happy ever after."

The weakest part of the novel is its denouement; the plot is also marred by a purely extraneous subplot involving a traveling showman, Anthony Flippance; his daughter, Polly; and their friends in the "theater" (a marionette show). The strength of the novel is its patient portrayal of the unknowingly eccentric country people whose names usually suggest their character. In addition to Jinny Boldero, a witty, strong-willed, somewhat sentimental, simple country girl, there are Will's mother, Martha Flynt, instinctively jealous of the woman who will marry her son; Will's gentle, simple old father; Jinny's irascible old grandfather, Daniel Quarles; a tract-bearing, mustachioed seamstress, Miss Gentry; a dirty old poaching shepherd, Uncle Lilliwhyte; and other memorable folk. They live undisturbed by the outside world. The name of their religion—Peculiar—suggests their insularity. The Peculiars, a faith-healing sect, is the dominant religion of Chipstone; and the existence of a skeptic (Bundock), a Methodist (Daniel Quarles), an Anglican (Miss Gentry), and a Christadelphian (Martha Flynt), creates the major conflict in their quiet lives. In spite of occasional squabbles over Bible texts, the final impression of them is of simple, goodhearted, deeply pious people, the kind that existed, as Zangwill says in the Preamble to the book, in "the Arcadian . . . days before the Deluge" (2).

## VIII  *In Summary*

It should be obvious from the foregoing discussions that Zangwill's major weakness as a novelist was in his failure to trim his all too prolific narratives. One critic's complaint (reflecting almost

every Zangwill critic's complaint) about *The Master* applies to
most of Zangwill's novels: "it is not so much too long as too
full." [26] When there is not too much going on, as in *The Mantle
of Elijah*, there is too much detail about the little going on, as
in *Jinny the Carrier*. In his best works, however, the abundance
of detail contributes to the effect of Realism, as in *Children of
the Ghetto* or in *The Master*; and in his worst novel, *The Mantle
of Elijah*, it is precisely the lack of detail and plot development
that is most missed.

Another major weakness of Zangwill as novelist is a tendency
toward a "rhapsodic" style, which usually fails because of stilted
diction, an overuse of apostrophe, and overelaborate sentence
patterns. Zangwill is also guilty occasionally of lapses into nineteenth-century pedantic diction and sentence structure at its worst.
I cite as an example the following illustrations from *Jinny the
Carrier*, which was written at the end of his career, when one
would expect him to have corrected the faults of the early style:
"His cranium was, in fact, like the advertisement of a hair-restorer
in the picture preceding the application thereof" (54); "Before
his eyes could return normally to their orbits or his breath to his
windpipe, the incredible vision had vanished" (134). Furthermore, Zangwill cannot resist epigrams and puns; favorite puns,
like "Methodism in his madness" or "let sleeping dogmas lie,"
appear more than once. On the other hand, his humor at its
best appears in his style in the form of reversals of clichés (as,
the veterinarian had "a good styside manner") and in thematic
epigrams (such as those cited from *The Mantle of Elijah*). Most
of the time, he writes a clear, vivid, though undistinguished, style.

His strength as novelist lay in the depiction of character and
in the suggestions of beauty in a real, oftentimes ugly, world.
Like the artist of *The Master*, Zangwill is at his best when he
is showing us ordinary life—whether that life is of the London
ghetto, London art circles, or rural Essex. Into his Realistic
milieu he characteristically places not the heroes and heroines
of romance but people we might actually meet: the "sweater,"
the school girl, the rich man's dilettantish son, the struggling
young artist, the simple country girl. Notable in Zangwill's
characterization is the fact that he seldom creates a wholly
despicable character (Bob Broser in *The Mantle of Elijah* is an
exception); he usually reveals the spiritual strength, the intel-

lectual agility, the unexpected kindness, or the sincere piety of even the meanest of mankind—in short, he finds a trace of human dignity in even the weakest of men.

Though Zangwill's best novels deal with life in the ghetto, the novels he wrote on non-Jewish themes show an ability to deal with a wide range of subjects and themes, including the absurdity of political life (*The Premier and the Painter*), the disillusioning pursuit of an ideal (*The Master*), the ruthlessness of modern politics (*The Mantle of Elijah*), and the simple lives and blind routine of rural life (*Jinny the Carrier*). We are impressed not only with the variety of themes but of forms: Zangwill wrote two political satires, two collections of sketches unified around the comic motif of marriage, a Realistic portrait of ghetto life, a comedy celebrating the triumph of a beggar-king in a world of rogues and fools, a Realistic portrait of the artist, and a "bland" novel designed to soothe its readers by depiction of a bygone age.

In the novels which are influenced by other literary work, Zangwill makes skillful use of his sources; in fact, *The Premier and the Painter* transcends its source, Twain's *The Prince and the Pauper*, in sophistication of character, plot, and satiric range; and *Children of the Ghetto* surpasses Mrs. Humphrey Ward's *Robert Elsmere* in depiction of character and philosophic depth. If *The King of Schnorrers* does not equal Jonson's *Alchemist*, it is at least another masterpiece in the tradition of Jonson's comic confidence man.

CHAPTER 4

# *"The Poetry of Mean Streets and Every-Day Figures"*

66 **A** single one of these tales is worth a dozen 'Masters,' "
a reviewer remarked of Zangwill's collection of short
stories entitled *"They that Walk in Darkness."* ¹ Though the critic
underestimated *The Master,* he was certainly right to recognize in
Zangwill's ghetto stories the work of a master. Some critics
think that Zangwill is at his best in the short-story form; and,
if *Children of the Ghetto* is viewed not as a novel but as "a
gallery of pictures drawn from life," as one critic² has described
it, and his *King of Schnorrers* is considered a long short story,
as its appearance in a volume of short stories would suggest,
we would have to agree. A significant number of Zangwill's
stories reveal the subtle characterization, controlled structure, and
world view of a sensitive and skilled artist.

Zangwill's short stories appeared in five collections: *Ghetto
Tragedies* (1893), containing the stories "Satan Mekatrig," "The
Diary of a *Meshummad,*" " 'Incurable,' " and "The Sabbath
Breaker"; *The King of Schnorrers: Grotesques and Fantasies*
(1894), containing, along with humorous or whimsical stories,
three ghetto stories; *"They that Walk in Darkness": Ghetto
Tragedies* (1899), which adds to the original *Ghetto Tragedies*
seven portraits of Jewish life; *The Grey Wig: Stories and Novel-
ettes* (1903), which contains stories not on Jewish subjects; and
*Ghetto Comedies* (1907), which, along with *"They that Walk in
Darkness,"* contains Zangwill's best stories.

With only a few exceptions, Zangwill's greatest skill lay in
depicting Jewish life, seen as neither unremittingly tragic or
comic, as the titles of two collections suggest, but as tragicomic,
encompassing both the joy and sadness of life. The ghetto
stories are not simply local-color stories. Some implicitly plead
for tolerance and brotherhood; others show the ironic or tragic
effects of loss of faith and tradition; still others analyze the failure

of Jews to realize (or even to recognize) common goals. The scope of the stories is large, ranging from the effects of a broken engagement to the devastation of a pogrom.

## I  Stories of Love and Sacrifice

Some of the stories are comic love and marriage stories, as for example, "A Rose of the Ghetto," "The Tug of Love," and "Holy Wedlock." "A Rose of the Ghetto," in *The King of Schnorrers: Grotesques and Fantasies*, follows a traditional comic pattern: the young lovers, assisted by Sugarman the Shadchan (the marriage broker from *Children of the Ghetto*), outwit the girl's unwilling father and gain both his consent to marry and a dowry. In "The Tug of Love" (*Ghetto Comedies*) young love and Sugarman again triumph: in devising a plan for young Goldenberg to get his engagement ring back from Fannie Ferscht, Sugarman actually arranges a reunion of the quarreling lovers; the tug on Fanny's ring finger which was to restore to Goldenberg his ring becomes instead an irresistible "tug of' love."

"Holy Wedlock," also in *Ghetto Comedies*, reverses the usual roles assigned youth and age in comedy: the lovers are an eighty-four-year-old grandmother, the *Bube* Yenta, and a seventy-five-year-old hunchback, Yossel Mandelstein; as *senex* is Schneemann, grandson of the *Bube*. The courtship of Yossel and the *Bube* is scandalizing the ghetto, so Schneemann, in the manner of a father buying off an unwanted suitor for his daughter, gives Yossel money to go away. But the only obstacle to the elopement of the old lovers was Yossel's refusal to take the grandmother's money. When he has the money for his own expenses, he and the grandmother marry and go to Jerusalem.

Parental love is another frequent subject of the ghetto stories. "The Sabbath Breaker" records a Polish grandmother's death-bed memory of "The one great episode of her life." [3] Once forty years ago she had broken the Sabbath to walk thirty-seven miles to attend her sick son, who died before she arrived; the story recounts the hardships of her journey. Such parental devotion is lacking in "Flutter-Duck" (in *The King of Schnorrers: Grotesques and Fantasies*), in which the mother causes her daughter's estrangement from the family. Whereas "The Sabbath Breaker" focuses on the character of the loving mother, "Flutter-

Duck" characterizes an empty-headed and vain mother, the "flutter-duck" of the title. Flutter-Duck is not satirized, however; she is made to appear pathetic in her unenlightened treatment of her daughter, her foolish vanity and pride, and her eventual reduction to the necessity of schnorring in the marketplace.

Another ignorant and pathetic mother is Zillah, of " 'They that Walk in Darkness,' " the first story in the collection of that name. After extensive fasting and praying, Zillah bears a child long after she and her husband have ceased hoping for one. The boy is brilliant, but sickly, and at thirteen goes blind. Zillah then begins to search for a cure for his blindness. When physicians declare the blindness incurable, she tries a desperate measure: on the advice of her Sabbath Fire-Woman, Zillah takes her son to the Pope in Rome for cure. The darkness of the title is a reference to both the boy's blindness and the mother's ignorance. As the story unfolds, it is clear that the mother's fasting two days a week during pregnancy is the cause of the boy's frail health; one doctor comments that the blindness is like that which comes after the great fasts in Russia.[4] Furthermore, she probably precipitates her son's early death by taking him on a long, fatiguing trip to Rome; on the day of the papal reception, the boy is ill, but she asks him to go with her to "the great healer," in whose presence the boy dies. Ironically, her piety and maternal concern destroy the child. Yet we are left with no horror at Zillah's deeds, only with pity for her helplessness and sorrow. For, just as the boy's darkness is filled with memories of the books he has studied and visions of the bright world about him, so the mother's darkness is filled with simple piety and great love.

In "Transitional," another parent-child story, the child comes to see the value of the parent's "darkness." The story develops one of Zangwill's favorite themes, that of the Hannah-David story in *Children of the Ghetto*, of filial sacrifice out of respect for the father's piety. The structure of "Transitional" is typical of Zangwill's longer stories and serves, therefore, as illustrative of his technical proficiency: the opening sections (I–V) move slowly, almost leisurely, providing exposition (of the Peyser family's life in Portsmouth before their move to London), characterization (of the pious father, gradually suppressed by six husband-seeking daughters and a wife determined to find bride-grooms for them all), and atmosphere (of the aggressive, woman-dominated London household in contrast with the less pretentious, father-dominated, religious household of the girls' childhood). Finally, all the daughters but the youngest, Schnapsie, are married; the mother dies, promising in her last words a husband for Schnapsie.

In the second part of the story (Secs. VI-IX) Daniel Peyser learns that his favorite, Schnapsie, is engaged to a Christian but that she will not marry for fear of hurting him; for the sake of his daughter's happiness, Daniel gives his consent to the marriage. To his distress, Schnapsie tells him that she plans to become a Christian, for "I believe in self-sacrifice; that is Christianity," whereas "We [Jews] have outlived our destiny. Our isolation is a meaningless relic." [5] As the day of the wedding nears, Daniel becomes increasingly troubled. He goes to a Christian wedding and—his mind wandering, anticipating Schnapsie's own wedding —forbids the banns. When Schnapsie reads of this strange incident in the paper, she realizes the extent of her father's sacrifice and breaks off her engagement because

If a religion that I thought all formalism is capable of producing such types of abnegation as my dear father, then it must, too, somewhere or other, hold in solution all those ennobling ingredients, all those stimuli to self-sacrifice, which the world calls Christian. . . . Perhaps the prosaic epoch of Judaism into which I was born is only transitional, perhaps it only belongs to the middle classes, for I know I felt more of its poetry in my childhood; perhaps the future will develop (or recultivate) its diviner sides and lay more stress upon the life beautiful, and thus all this blind instinct of isolation may prove only the conservation of the race for its nobler future, when it may still become, in very truth, a witness to the Highest, a chosen people in whom all the families of the earth may be blessed.[6]

The climax of the story is, like the rest of it, subdued; it consists of Schnapsie's reading a newspaper item and realizing its significance. The theme of self-sacrifice controls the story: in the first part, the father relinquishes his community and family importance so that his daughters can find husbands; in the second part, he willingly suppresses his disapproval of the Christian marriage so that Schnapsie can be happy. The story is resolved as Schnapsie proves worthy of the father's sacrifice by giving up her marriage.

Self-sacrifice is also the theme of " 'Incurable' " in *Ghetto Tragedies*. In this story, set in the ghetto hospital for incurables, one of the patients learns that, in her absence, her husband has taken another woman. So that he will not live in sin, the wife demands that he divorce her. At the end of the story, she is heartbroken and desolate, having just blessed her husband's new wife. Her generosity is given wider application by the final words of the story, uttered by the saintly Sister Margaret, who wishes that she could "die for" the agonized woman with palsy in the ward above.

A woman does die for others in "The Keeper of Conscience" (in *"They that Walk in Darkness"*), a heavily ironic story in which the self-sacrifice is not only unappreciated but despised. A young, girl, Salvina Brill, outraged when her father leaves her mother for another woman, spends the rest of her life working to support the mother. In accord with her strict conscience, Salvina disapproves of a possible money-marriage for her sister; and she objects when her brother begins accepting money from the prospering father. Salvina works herself to death, dying unlamented in her mid-twenties. After her death, the family is free to do as it likes—the lazy brother to live off his father; the sister to marry her rich, vulgar suitor; and the mother to return to her repentant husband. The mother's final words are Salvina's epitaph, "She did spoil our lives for years." [7] The suggestion is that Salvina's pride and conscientiousness are too much for most humans, who prefer a more selfish, more comfortable, and less exacting existence. Salvina wastes herself and her family in her mistaken though noble attempts to save them from lapses in conscience.

## II  *Stories of Suffering, Guile, and Hope*

The hard life of the ghetto is the subject of many of these stories, but nowhere is it so pronounced as in "The Red Mark" (*Ghetto Comedies*), which depicts the hard-working, essentially joyless life of a child in the ghetto. The red mark is given each child for punctuality in school; the conflict in the story is little Bloomah Beckenstein's struggle to get to school on time, or to

get to school at all; for she is kept out of school to assist her
mother or married sisters when they need help. A major joy
in her life is a banner given at the Ghetto Board School to the
class with the best weekly attendance; at the end of the story,
her class possesses the banner for that week, and she is "happiest
of a radiant sisterhood." In "The Red Mark," Bloomah's life is
portrayed as relentlessly severe, but the ghetto provides goals and
a milieu with which she can identify. All the children of the
ghetto in Zangwill's stories are presented sympathetically but
not sentimentally.

Some of the children of the ghetto are capable of cleverness
or guile. In the vein of *The King of Schnorrers*, Zangwill has
in *Ghetto Comedies* three confidence-man stories. In "The Model
of Sorrows" a Christian artist comes to understand Jewish character through his attempts to paint Christ after a Jewish model,
Israel Quarriar, "a frowsy, gaberdined Jew" with a noble, stooped
figure and a "tragic face." The artist first paints the dignity and
suffering in the face of his model; but, as he becomes familiar
with Israel's character, his portrait of Christ changes. The five
parts of the story show the artist's gradual comprehension of
Israel's nature. "How I Found the Model" shows Israel at the
Brighton Church parade, where he strikingly contrasts with the
well-dressed Jews. "The Model's Story," from Israel's point of
view, tells of the sufferings of him and his family in making an
escape from Russia; this chapter introduces the confidence-man
motif as Israel tells how he was cheated by a fellow Jew. "The
Picture Evolves" has the artist realize, as a result of Israel's
story, that Christ is "incarnated in a race, suffering . . . in its
Passion."

In "I Become a Sorter," the artist attempts to set Israel up
in business as a sorter of tailor's scraps; the title becomes symbolic
when the artist, for the first time suspecting that Israel may be
a cheat, is faced with the problem of sorting lies from truth.
"Last Stage of All" confirms the artist's suspicions, as Israel
refuses to appear with his family at a hearing to vindicate his
good name. The artist now envisions a "new Man of Sorrows"
and adds a "look of craft and guile" to the portrait, which then
becomes "nearly . . . a photographic representation" of Israel.
Finally, he hopes that "this return to a truer homeliness and a
more real realism did but enable me to achieve a subtler beauty.

For surely here at last was the true tragedy of the people of Christ—to have persisted sublimely, and to be as sordidly perverted; to be king and knave in one." [8]

The character of the Jew as "king and knave in one" is also seen in "The Luftmensch," where an artist, Leopold Barstein, is besieged by the florid rhetoric of Nehemiah Silvermann, seen by Barstein as "an air-man, floating on facile wings through the aether." Though the poverty of Silvermann and his family is real enough, Barstein concludes that Silvermann has "mainly dictionary distresses, felt most keenly in the rhapsody of literary composition." [9] Silvermann becomes to Barstein an incarnation of "the great Jewish gospel of the improvident lilies" and, as such, continues to get money from Barstein and his friends.

A variation of the confidence-man story is "The Yiddish 'Hamlet,'" which has as protagonist the poet of *Children of the Ghetto*, Melchitsedek Pinchas. Pinchas has improved Shakespeare by translating *Hamlet* "into modern terms." He has omitted the ghost and made Hamlet Hebrew; "the play is virtually an autobiography," Pinchas explains. [10] Pinchas gets Goldwater's Yiddish theater to produce the play, a tragedy of "the internal incapacity of the thinker for the lower activity of action" (298). The climactic moment arrives as Pinchas, horrified to see his tragedy turned into a Passover play complete with Ghost, an aging Ophelia, songs, and street vernacular, rushes enraged onto the stage to beat the "Prince of Palestine" with his cane. The story ends as it began, at a café where Pinchas reverses his earlier position to say that "Action is greater than Thought" (332).

In addition to these stories, which seem primarily designed to provide glimpses into Jewish character, are those designed to convey a message. Stories pleading—not overtly, but dramatically —for religious tolerance are "A Tragi-Comedy of Creeds" (in *The King of Schnorrers: Grotesques and Fantasies*) and "The Bearer of Burdens" (*Ghetto Comedies*). In the former, a poor workingman, himself an atheist, asks a rabbi whom he encounters on the street to administer last rites to his dying wife, a Protestant Christian. The workingman checks only to be sure that the clergyman is not Roman Catholic; he is satisfied with a rabbi, explaining, "If you believe in God, that's enough, ain't it? You're both religious folk." The rabbi reads the deathbed confession in English to the dying woman, as a Roman Catholic doctor and the atheist husband look on. The woman dies, "the three men becoming as little children in the presence of the eternal mystery." [11]

The brotherhood of men of differing religions is again illustrated by "The Bearer of Burdens," in which a child with a Christian mother becomes the most dutiful and affectionate grandchild of an old-clothes woman, a Jewess, Natalya. Natalya's son-in-law marries three times: first, Natalya's daughter, by whom he has two children; then a Christian, who loves and cares for the first wife's children and who has one child of her own; finally a Jewess, who beats the children and drinks. From the third wife Natalya rescues all three children, taking pity on the blue-eyed child of the Christian woman. Natalya's own grandchildren leave her as soon as they are old enough; Daisy, the Christian's child, stays to comfort and love Natalya. At the end of the story, the Christian grandmother has found her grandchild and Natalya dies, saying a Hebrew prayer, with Daisy repeating a Christian verse taught her by her new-found grandmother.

### III    Stories of Sabbath Breaking, Apostasy, and Assimilation

Many of Zangwill's stories with religious themes are concerned with the collapse of orthodox Judaism, which represents in the stories, as it does in *Children of the Ghetto*, not only religious rigidity and formalism but also family stability and piety; therefore, the gradual collapse of orthodoxy becomes symbolic of an adjustment to a new society and of a weakening of old values. Invariably, Zangwill reveals in his stories that the price of adjustment, of "Anglicization," as the title of one story has it, is high. Often the doubter or the convert to Christianity returns to Judaism because of childhood memories or familial affection.

One of the forms of adjustment/collapse involves Sabbath-breaking, which constitutes the subject of several of Zangwill's stories. In "The Land of Promise" (in *"They that Walk in Darkness"*) Srul immigrates to America, for he cannot earn a living in Russia because he refuses to work on the Sabbath. Four women—Srul's mother, his fiancée, and her sisters—wait for years for Srul to earn enough to send for them. Srul is finally prosperous enough, but his fiancée is denied entry into the United

States because of an eye disease. She manages to slip into the country through Canada, only to find when she arrives that Srul has married her young, healthy sister. The story contrasts the patient, aging fiancée with the hustling Srul, who has found America "the land of enlightenment and freedom." He wants the young sister as his wife not only because she is prettier and healthier but because she does not disapprove of his keeping his shop open on the Sabbath. To see the collapse of values implicit in Srul's Sabbath-breaking, we may contrast his motives with the old woman's in "The Sabbath Breaker": he profanes the Sabbath to make money; she, to visit her dying son. Srul's willingness to break the Sabbath is accompanied by his willingness to behave selfishly and cruelly to his old love.

"The Sabbath Question in Sudminster" (*Ghetto Comedies*) is a comic treatment of the subject; in the story, Simeon Samuels offends the pious Jews of Sudminster by keeping his shop open on the Sabbath. The congregation tries to stop Samuels, who in his witty defenses and shrewd dealings with the opposition equals the King of Schnorrers. The congregation begins its crusade by having the minister preach against Sabbath-breaking. Pleas and arguments failing, the merchants finally resort to buying Samuels' stock. But Samuels simply advertises that he has sold his "old-fashioned stock" and is getting new. Finally, in desperation, they open their shops on Saturday to compete with him. This last measure succeeds in driving Samuels away; but, after he leaves, the Sudminster merchants continue to open their shops on Saturday. As in "The Land of Promise," the desire for material gain overcomes the pious inclinations of the congregation; in both stories, the rigid refusal to admit profanation of the Sabbath ironically leads to habitual Sabbath-breaking and to an implicit collapse of values.

Just as Sabbath-breaking is a recurrent subject in Zangwill's stories, so is the *Meshummad* (apostate) a recurrent character. Two of Zangwill's *Ghetto Tragedies* have protagonists who have fallen away from Judaism. "Satan Mekatrig" shows the perversion of Moshé Grinwitz by a "black-coated, fur-capped, red-haired hunchback," whom Moshé's wife identifies as the Satan Mekatrig. Through the influence of this evil companion, Moshé becomes a skeptic and denies his pious wife, Rebecca. The wife, however, is the means of his salvation; as Moshé is dying,

Rebecca returns to him with a baby, their child; and Moshé dies in her care, clutching his child, "my *Kaddish*!"

In this story the principle of evil—represented by the mysterious stranger—is doubt, skepticism, and the temptation to convert to Christianity for gold. The values of the story—represented by Rebecca—are family and race—Judaism. When the Satan Mekatrig first appears to Moshé in the synagogue (Sec. I), the stranger's blasphemy and heresy are stopped by a child's saying *Kaddish*; Moshé is then saved (Sec. II) by his wife's piety. When he is tempted by the stranger to tear the mezuzah from his door, Moshé is stopped by the sound of his wife's saying the psalms; the stranger leaves, and Moshé and Rebecca finish the Sabbath prayer. However, Moshé lapses once more (Sec. III), and on the Day of Atonement, Rebecca's last hope for his salvation disappears, as she finds him at home with the stranger. When Moshé denies that she is his wife, she leaves him in eerie darkness. In a transitional section of the story (IV), Rebecca goes to the synagogue of Love and Mercy to pray, where she dreams of a heavenly service in which she is reunited with her family, which includes the Jewish patriarchs. This section, asserting in a vision the kinship of all Jews and the glorious heritage and future of the race, prepares for Moshé's final return to the faith. In the final section of the story (V), Moshé's family, his wife and child, redeem him.

Though Moshé is a skeptic, he refuses to convert to Christianity for money, as the hunchback has. But the second of the *Ghetto Tragedies*, "The Diary of a *Meshummad*," concerns a Jew who has converted to Christianity. The protagonist, a Russian widower, writes out of his need to confess his longings for his old faith. He grieves for his son, Paul, who is a Christian fanatic; in fact, Paul's book defending the Orthodox church wins him the editorship of an anti-Semitic journal. In the form of successive diary entries, the story falls into three parts: the first, covering about six weeks of entries, shows the father's return to Judaism and his estrangement from his son. In this section the father receives his first glimpse into Paul's anti-Semitism when his son sends him "a pronouncement on the Jewish question, venomous, scathing, mordant, terrific." [12] He also discovers that Paul has fallen in love with a Jewess but has rejected her.

The second part, beginning one year later, reveals the disastrous effects of the father's apostasy. The father tells his son that he is wealthy and need not edit the anti-Semitic paper. But Paul refuses his father's money, saying that the riches would have helped him earlier, when he needed money to marry; for Paul and the Jewish girl were kept apart not only by Paul's Christianity but by his poverty. In the third part of the story, six months later, the writer hears that a pogrom is in progress, with a mob shouting Paul's words; he decides to join his friend, Rabbi Isaac, and writes in the closing lines, "I go to proclaim the Unity." Thus the son unknowingly destroys the father, just as the father, by pretending to be a Christian and by concealing his wealth, had earlier, but unintentionally, destroyed the son.

Another story dealing with the repentant apostate and the conflict of parent and child is "To Die in Jerusalem" (in *"They that Walk in Darkness"*). In this story the son breaks from Judaism and achieves some fame as a playwright; but he finally returns, sick and penniless, to his father. The widowed father, however, forsaken by his son, has gone to Jerusalem to die. When he learns that his son is dying and begging for his forgiveness, he returns to England. But the son, summoning all his strength, has gone to Jerusalem to join the father. So the old man dies in London, content that his son died in Jerusalem.

The return to the faith also appears in "Elijah's Goblet" (*Ghetto Comedies*), in which a Jewish community is saved from a pogrom by the repentance of Maimon the *Meshummad*. The first part of this story (Secs. I-II) describes the *Seder* ceremony at Aaron Ben Amram's house. The mother, who fears a pogrom, does not want her husband to open the door for the ceremonial welcome to the prophet Elijah. But Aaron Ben Amram insists; and, as he flings open the door, Maimon runs in, escaping from a Christian mob. The second section of the story (Sec. III) is set in the synagogue the next day. The Passover liturgy is interrupted by Cossacks, who believe that they will find a lost Christian child's blood in the consecration wine bottle; failing to find anything but wine, they leave.

Then Ben Amram reveals to the congregation a plot: Maimon was to change a bottle of blood for the bottle of wine, thus giving the Christians a cause for the slaughter of Jews. But as Maimon left the synagogue on the *Seder*, Christians saw him and pursued him. Maimon was rescued by Ben Amram; and, seeing the *Seder* table, "his child-soul came back to him," and he confessed the plot to Ben Amram. "Elijah's Goblet" refers to the ceremonial goblet on the *Seder* table, reserved for Elijah, the precursor of the messiah; the significance of the title is clear when we note Ben Amram's conclusion: "God sends the Prophet of Redemption in strange guise." [13] It was Maimon the *Meshummad* who rushed in when the door was opened; it was he who, fainting, drank the wine from Elijah's goblet; it was he who, by confessing, saved the Jews from a pogrom.

"Anglicization" does not contain a *Meshummad* (apostate), but it shows the assimilation of the S. Cohns (the Solomon Cohens) into English society. The elder Cohns, prosperous and powerful in Sudminster, are eager to become Anglicized without actually giving up Judaism. When they move to London, their son, Simon, becomes thoroughly Anglicized; he falls in love with a Christian. At the end of the story, S. Cohn is dead; the Christian girl, Lucy, has rejected Simon because he is a Jew; and Simon has returned heartbroken to his mother. The thirteen sections of the story fall into three parts dealing with (1) the Cohns' attempts to become Englishmen as well as Jews; (2) the Boer War years, during which the Cohns lose their son to England; and (3) Simon's love affair after the war, when he discovers that he has retained enough of his Jewish identity to be rejected by Lucy. In this story Zangwill suggests that some aspects of Judaism resist assimilation: the son's horror at the idea of becoming a *Meshummad*; the fact of English anti-Semitism, represented here by Lucy's anti-alien father; and the mother's protective love for her injured son, which, according to the last line of the story, has been "saved from Anglicization."

Another assimilated Jew who finds that he cannot emancipate himself from anti-Semitism is Rozenoffski, the pianist-protagonist of "The Hirelings." The setting is on shipboard as Rozenoffski returns from an unsuccessful American tour; he is outraged at the "narrow-souled anti-Semites" who assumed that he was Jewish and that he "did not share their aversion from the gaberdine or the three brass balls."[14] But he meets a beautiful Jewess, who plans to return to Russia to help her people; and he is persuaded by her fervid allegiance to join her. Under her inspiration, he begins to play daily concerts for himself; these concerts attract large and appreciative audiences on shipboard; and his final performance, a "synagogue medley," wins him an audience with the woman who had refused to receive him in Chicago. At the end of the story, Rozenoffski is denying his Jewishness for the sake of acceptance and possible fame. He feels that he has "burst the coils" of "narrow tribalism," but he has in reality become a "hireling," the kind of Jewish genius condemned earlier by the girl: "Never a song of Israel do they fashion, nor a picture of Israel, nor a law of Israel, nor a temple of Israel. Bah! What are they but hirelings?" (419)

Denial of Judaism as the price of success is also the theme of "The Converts" (in *Ghetto Comedies*). Elkan Mandle is ruined when he deserts his wife and children to elope with the beautiful Gittel Goldstein. Gittel becomes a successful actress, leaves Elkan, and becomes famous as "Yvonne Rupert." The story opens as Elkan, in poverty on the New York Bowery, is pasting pictures of Yvonne on boxes of the "Yvonne Rupert cigar"; he recognizes Gittel in these pictures and tries to see her, but she refuses to recognize him. In the transitional sections (V–VI) Elkan is in jail, where a service for Jewish prisoners on the Day of Atonement makes him resolve to go home again. His attempt at reconciliation with his wife, Haigitcha, fails (Sec. VII); rather than starve, he converts to Christianity and makes a living preaching (Sec. VIII). The story closes with Zangwill's bitterly ironic comment: "And so, while Haigitcha walks in darkness, Yvonne prays in her chapel and Elkan preaches in the church."

Zangwill clearly does not like the "hireling" who acts out of selfish motives, betraying himself and his people; and he just as clearly defends the unenlightened "darkness" of family ties and conscience in which his Jews walk. He also dislikes the anti-Semitism implicit in "Anglicization," in emancipation from the "narrow tribalism" of the Jews. Rosenoffski in "The Hirelings" is as much an anti-Semite as the Americans who refused to hear him. And in another story, "The Jewish Trinity," a Jewish artist, Barstein, is rejected as suitor for Sir Asher Aaronsberg's daughter because Barstein is a Zionist. Sir Asher and his daughter are horrified at the notion of living in a "Ghetto" (Palestine) "entirely among Jews!" [15] Ironically, Sir Asher was the inspiration for Barstein's return to Judaism.

At a dinner party for English upper-class society given by Sir Aaron (depicted in Secs. I-II), Barstein revises his opinion of Sir Aaron: the man whom Barstein considered the epitome of English imperialist opinion utters a long Hebrew prayer at the dinner table, the words of which instill in the cynical Barstein "a racial pride." Inspired by Sir Aaron and his beautiful daughter, who to Barstein incarnates Jewish aspiration, beauty, and mystery, Barstein joins the Zionists (Sec. III). Barstein courts the daughter, who agrees to marry him but not to live in Palestine (Sec. IV); but Sir Aaron rejects Barstein, on the grounds that he is impious (to Judaism), traitorous (to England), and disrespectful (to Sir Aaron) (Sec. V). These accusations arise when Barstein observes that Jews like Sir Aaron individually constitute a trinity: "the Briton, the Jew, and the anti-Semite—three-in-one and one-in-three" (135).

### IV   Stories of Dreams that Fail

Another story anatomizing Jewish failure is "Noah's Ark" (in *"They that Walk in Darkness"*); it depicts the collapse of a territorialist ideal because of the "pious patience" of the Jews, which places "the burden [of salvation of the Jews] on to the shoulders of Messiah and Miracle."[16] In this story the protagonist, Peloni (his name is a Hebrew word meaning "a certain one"), aspires to establish a Jewish homeland. He is lured to New York by an advertisement in which Mordecai Manuel Noah proclaims a Jewish nation in the New World; Noah plans to establish the land of Ararat on Grand Island (near Niagara Falls) and commissions Peloni to plant the flag there. Peloni stays on the island through the winter, waiting for the arrival of Noah and other Jewish pilgrims. When spring comes, Peloni hears that Noah has now chosen Palestine, not Ararat, for the Jews' homeland. At the climax of the story, Peloni recognizes a brotherhood with Red Jacket, an American Indian who, puzzled by Peloni's winter wait, asks why he builds "a monument but never a city"; leaving the island with Red Jacket, Peloni realizes that they are "both doomed."[17] In despair, Peloni throws himself into the falls. The story dramatizes Zangwill's conviction that the "pious patience" which allows the Jew to tolerate persecution and the Zionist zeal which makes him unable to accept any home but Palestine are suicidal.

The Jews' wait for "Messiah and Miracle" is the subject of

another story in *"They that Walk in Darkness."* "Bethulah" portrays a maiden who represents to the narrator the "undying, ever re- juvenescent hope" of Judaism. Bethulah (whose name means "virgin" in Hebrew) is the daughter of a rabbi in a small Euro- pean village, Zloczszol; she appears first to the narrator as a vision of the Holy Queen Sabbath. He grows to love the "mystic moonlit figure" and asks to marry her; but he is refused because her Hassidic cult believes that she is to give birth to the messiah. The last sections of the story (VIII–IX) shift to events fifty years later, when the narrator, after a happy life, is reminded of his youthful love by a newspaper item. He travels back to Zloczszol and finds Bethulah there, aging but still beautiful. She professes to be faithful to her dream; but in the last scene she is found asleep over a Bible in her cottage, where she has been reading in Genesis the Lord's assurance that Sarah, though old, can bear a child. The story implicitly contrasts Bethulah's sterile, wasted life devoted to a lofty spiritual ideal with the life of fulfillment and contentment led by the narrator, who married and had children. Like "Noah's Ark," this story suggests that the Jews' willingness to wait for a miraculous deliverance is self-destructive; Bethulah's followers are now skeptics, and she clings to a futile, though beautiful, hope.

There is no beauty in Zangwill's analysis of Jewish failure in "Samooborona," the last story in *Ghetto Comedies.* Zangwill wrote in the introductory note to *Ghetto Comedies* that he "ven- tured to disregard" the traditional notion that a happy ending distinguishes comedy from tragedy and that this disregard is especially evident in the last story. Certainly "Samooborona," which ends with the protagonist's suicide during a massive pogrom, has nothing of the comic about it. The story is a ferocious satire on the self-destructive factionalism of the Jews. It is set in a Russian town, Milovka, where young David Ben Amram goes to organize a *Samooborona* (Self-Defense) against a pogrom planned for the town. He is unsuccessful, for the populace refuses to arm or to support armed resistance. David finds in Milovka internal arguments and rival political parties, each convinced that it repre- sents the "unconditional historic necessity," a phrase which be- comes a refrain as David vainly searches for some concern for mutual welfare. Even the children are partisans of numerous fac- tions, and the *Beth Hamedrash* (Institute of Learning) does not provide relief from party politics. Finally the pogrom arrives, but "in a new form"—artillery lined up to fire at the Jewish quarter. Just before David kills himself, he "felt grimly that an economic Providence had saved him from wasting his time in training pistoliers." The final paragraphs describe the devastation of the ghetto and end with Zangwill's grim observation that "The same unconditional historic necessity had overtaken them all." [18]

## V  Stories on Non-Jewish Subjects

When Zangwill turns to non-Jewish subjects, his work is seldom artistically satisfying; the non-Jewish stories are, for the most part, mildly amusing but not impressive, though they were often popular successes. One of the early successes was a detective story, *The Big Bow Mystery,* which appeared serially in the *London Star* in 1891, was published separately in 1892, and was reprinted in *The Grey Wig: Stories and Novelettes.* This "locked-door" murder mystery depicts the gradual accumulation of evidence pointing to a murder suspect named Mortlake; the shady alliance of a retired Scotland Yard detective, Grodman, and a journalist who has ghost-written Grodman's *Criminals I Have Caught;* the trial and conviction of Mortlake; and the final surprise confession of detective Grodman.

A series of ironies make the story a better-than-average example of its genre: Grodman, the detective-murderer, planned a "perfect crime" in order to confound his rival at Scotland Yard; but his rival instead gains renown for finding the presumed killer, Mortlake. Grodman then confesses, not to save Mortlake, but to destroy the rival's reputation; however, after he confesses, he discovers that Mortlake has just established an alibi and been reprieved, thus making Grodman's confession superfluous. Evidence of the popularity of *The Big Bow Mystery* is the fact that it has been filmed three times: as *The Perfect Crime* (FBO Productions, Inc., 1928), as *Crime Doctor* (Radio-Keith-Orpheum Radio Pictures, 1934), and as *The Verdict* (Warner Brothers Pictures, Inc., 1946); in the latter Sydney Greenstreet played Grodman and Peter Lorre played the journalist-conspirator.

Two stories in *The King of Schnorrers: Grotesques and Fantasies* are also murder stories. "The Memory Clearing House" is a fantasy about a man who establishes a clearing house for unwanted memories. The narrator, a novelist who wants to paint a "veracious picture of life," uses an authentic memory from the clearing house as material for a novel about a murder. The critics, like all critics in Zangwill's stories, are totally mistaken in their estimate of the novel; when they complain of its tameness and improbability, the angered writer tells them that the novel is based on fact. The police investigate the case; and, as a result, the narrator is writing the story as a condemned prisoner. The tone of this story is light: the narrator is confident that he will be released, and his last words are a pun—"If I am reprieved, I will never buy another murderer's memory. . . . I'll be hanged if I do." [19]

"Cheating the Gallows," a better mystery story, presents a dapper bank manager and an unkempt journalist, who are roommates. The bank manager disappears with bank money, forsaking his sweetheart, who is then wooed and won by the journalist. Just before the marriage, however, the girl dreams that the journalist murdered his roommate; after a search, the police find the banker's body in the river and the bank's money in the journalist's possession. The last section of the story, "Brief Résumé of the Culprit's Confession," reveals that the banker and journalist were the same man—a quick-change artist who planned the double identity in order to commit the bank robbery. His plan failed only because his fiancée had a fantastic dream (and a thief stole the banker's clothes). The elements of suspense and surprise in this story make it an interesting, though trivial, story.

Almost all the short stories in *The King of Schnorrers: Grostesque and Fantasies* are trivial in subject, and some are clumsy in form. Romantic love is the theme of "Mated by a Waiter" and "The Principal Boy." The former is primarily notable for its portrait of a comic waiter who in his clever control of others foreshadows Sir James Barrie's Admirable Crichton; and "The Principal Boy," for its portrait of the unsentimental heroine, who achieves independence by becoming an actress, specifically playing the principal boy in the pantomine. Two of the stories in this collection satirize the literary world: "An Honest Log-Roller" features a novelist turned critic after he loses the only copy of his first novel. After he becomes a famous critic for the *Acadaeum* (Zangwill's parody of the names of two influential literary magazines, *The Academy* and *The Athenaeum*), he discovers through a friend that in one review he has slated his own lost novel. He also discovers that what he praises his readers avoid and what he condemns they read; as a result, the critic's novel becomes a popular success. He finds the thief; they divide the profits; the thief writes a second novel. "And the critic slated it. And they divided the profits." [20]

"A Double-Barrelled Ghost" seems written for the sake of a pun: a young man, having suffered a sudden loss of fortune, sees the ghost of his great-grandfather, who advises his descendant to publish a hidden manuscript. When the obvious pun on ghost-writing has been exhausted (from overwork), the humor in the story derives from Zangwill's satire on literary critics. The hidden manuscript, entitled *The Learned Pig,* is a contemporary's attack on Samuel Johnson; the critics praise the book for its brilliant portrait of Johnson's greatness and attack it for its anachronisms and artificial conversations.

Three stories of *The King of Schnorrers: Grotesques and Fantasies* are humorous variations of legends. In "The Semi-Sentimental Dragon," the dragon rescues the lady from a lecherous Saint George. The dragon is a stage one, and Saint George is the manager of a theater and the star of a pantomime. The rear half of the dragon falls in love with the heroine, and, outraged at the manager's treatment of her, tramples him during a performance. "Santa Claus. A Story for the Nursery" is a Christmas story about a ragged child who thinks that, if he has a stocking to hang up, he will get presents, as prosperous children do. Instead of the sentimental ending, which we might expect from this situation, there is a cynically humorous one in which the boy miraculously obtains stockings (though a fat woman drowns in the process) and then finds them filled on Christmas morning with Spanish lace (which the boy sells) and cigars (which he smokes). "The Queen's Triplets. A Nursery Tale for the Old" parodies the fairy-tale search for the king's heir. While his two brothers go out to slay a dragon to prove their worth, the third brother stays home and courts the princess; for his efforts, he eventually wins the princess and the kingdom; but the two brothers return without having "scotched the serpent"; indeed, without even having found it.

Other stories in this collection are harder to classify: "An Odd Life," a whimsical story with a serious theme, features a man who lives only the even years of his life and then is reborn to live the odd years (hence the title). As he is dying of croup in his second life, he realizes that he has led a wasted as well as an odd life: he dissipated his first lifetime counting on a second, and his second holds no promise or surprise for him. "Vagaries of a Viscount" is neither a good humorous story nor a good mystery story; the narrator, Paul Pry (of *The Bachelors' Club*), follows a viscount and tries to make sense of his disguises and strange adventures. Finally Paul discovers that there is no sense to them, for the viscount, mistaking his friend Pry for a hired detective, has been trying to mislead his shadow. To these unclassifiable stories may be added "A Successful Operation," the meaning of which escapes me. The principal characters are a newlywed couple and the young groom's father. When the father goes blind, the young wife insists that he have an eye operation in their own home, where she attends him lovingly. The operation is a success, and the old man's sight is restored. The final line is "When her [the young wife's] child was born it was blind."

Of considerably more merit are some of the stories in *The Grey Wig,* especially the title story. "The Grey Wig" is a touching story about two old ladies, Madame Dépine and Madame Valière, who cannot afford gray wigs and consequently must suffer the embarrassment of wearing brown wigs, inappropriate at their age. When the proprietess of their boardinghouse appears in a gray wig, the two ladies are drawn together. They become friends and, by numerous economies, eventually save enough money for one wig, for which they draw lots. Though Madame Dépine is the winner, she generously has the wig made for her friend, who has been invited to her nephew's wedding, a big occasion in her life. But the fact that one has a wig damages their friendship: Madame Dépine loses her freedom to go out with her friends, for "they might now have served as an advertisement. . . . Before the grey wig—after the grey wig." [21]

The ladies part when Madame Valière goes off to the wedding wearing the wig and Madame Dépine's gold brooch. When Madame Valière does not return, Madame Dépine suspects her of robbery, only to discover her old friend at the morgue and to realize, too late, that, compared to her "great yearning for love and reconciliation," the "grey wig seemed a petty and futile aspiration." [22] The wig is the central symbol in the story; it is the means for uniting, and then dividing, the old ladies; it causes both noble sacrifice and then jealousy and mean suspicions. To the old ladies, it represents the *convenable;* finally, too late, Madame Dépine realizes that it means less than friendship.

Another story about two proud old ladies is "The Silent Sisters." The first sentence of the story gives the situation: "They had quarrelled in girlhood, and mutually declared their intention never to speak to each other again."[23] A brief expository section traces the joys and sorrows of their lives; most of the story deals with one sister's care for her dying sister. Though the two women speak only through a third person because of their girlhood vow, their love for each other is revealed in subtle details. Other stories skillfully delineating womanly character are "The Woman Beater," with its exasperatingly petulant, greedy, self-willed, changeable heroine, and "The Eternal Feminine," with its long-suffering, patient, good-humored, hard-working, loving, but hopelessly ugly heroine.

"The Serio-Comic Governess" is also an ambitious attempt at character portrayal, but the central character, the governess, does not engage one's sympathies. She is supposed to combine exuberant wit with pious soul-searching, but her wit is often merely archly clever and her soul-searching unconvincing. From the time that her "mocking spirit" shocks the sisters at a convent school to the present of the story, when she is both governess and music hall entertainer, she leads a double life. The major conflict in the story is her attempt to be made "one with myself," a conflict which is not resolved by her accepting any of her numerous suitors but by her returning to her childhood resolve to enter a nunnery where she can have "my complex corrupt soul . . . simplified and purified,"[24] an unpersuasive solution in view of the mocking, irreverent strain in her character.

Though we cannot securely speak of stories of character and stories of plot since Henry James's "Art of Fiction," the dichotomy is a useful one in discussing Zangwill's short stories, some of which are primarily character revelation and some of which rely for their effect on Zangwill's manipulation of incident. "Chassé-Croisé" is of the latter sort; in this story an American heiress, Amber Roan, and a politically ambitious, poor Englishman, Walter Bassett, marry: she, for love; he, for ambition. Eventually, Bassett has a change of heart and resigns his cabinet post; but he discovers to his dismay that Amber has learned to like the feeling of power. The irony of the criss-cross is like that of the story, "Merely Mary Ann," which also involves a change of heart. In

"Merely Mary Ann" a snobbish composer comes to love a humble serving girl, only to realize finally that he is unworthy of her love.[25]

## VI  *A Singer of Israel*

In generalizing about Zangwill's achievement as a short-story writer, one must agree with the critic who said that "When Mr. Zangwill writes about his own people, though it be only to scourge or ridicule, he discards that air of jaunty flippancy which he deems appropriate to discussion of the rest of the universe." [26] If at times he abandons the "jaunty flippancy" to show us two lonely old women in Paris, or two stubborn, loving sisters, or an ugly woman made beautiful by the tenderness of unrequited love, if at times he gives us glimpses of the power of love, the beauty of self-sacrifice, or the perversion of ambition, too often in discussing "the rest of the universe" Zangwill uses techniques that are convention-worn, themes that are stale, or characters that have no life. Even the humor is different. It is illuminating to contrast the farcical action of "The Semi-Sentimental Dragon" with the hilarious version of *Hamlet* in "A Yiddish *Hamlet*." What a difference between the trouncing of the manager by the stage dragon and the mutilation of Pinchas' play as Mrs. Goldstein (Ophelia) piously waves the *Lulov* palm and Hamlet's mother says to the Prince of Palestine, "You have too many dead flies on you. . . . You'll get left." [27] Zangwill is unquestionably at his best when he follows the advice in his story "The Hirelings" and sings a song of Israel. Like the Jewish pianist who wins recognition for his "synagogue medley," Zangwill deserves greatest praise for his ghetto stories.

These stories together form an integrated view of world Jewry. To achieve the effect of coherence, Zangwill frequently provides in a story allusions to characters or events in other stories. For example, the central character of "The Sabbath Breaker" is one of the patients described in the exposition of " 'Incurable' "; S. Cohn, who with his son is central in "Anglicization," is alluded to in numerous stories, including "The Sabbath Question in Sudminster," where he is mentioned as the pious father-in-law of one of the congregation and in "The Bearer of Burdens," where Natalya's son-in-law is bookkeeper for S. Cohn's Clothing Emporium. Sir Aaron Aaronsberg, the anti-Semitic Jew of "The

Jewish Trinity," helps the Christian protagonist of "The Model of Sorrows" to find work for Israel Quarrier; and the artist Barstein, the rejected suitor of "The Jewish Trinity," appears as protagonist in "The Luftmensch," where he is the object of Nehemiah Silvermann's confidence game. The artists sharing Barstein's delight in Nehemiah's letter at the end of "The Luftmensch" themselves become the protagonists of other stories: Schneemann tries to separate the old lovers in "Holy Wedlock," and Rosenoffski prostitutes his art in "The Hirelings." So too the hero of "Samooborona," David Ben Amram, is mentioned as the red-haired Jewess' cousin in "The Hirelings"; and he appears as a child in "Elijah's Goblet."

Other cross-references are to characters and motifs in *Children of the Ghetto*. For example, the Benjy/Moses and Levi/Shemuel stories in *Children of the Ghetto* are retold in "To Die in Jerusalem"; Hannah's sacrifice for her father is duplicated in the daughter's sacrifice in "Transitional"; the attitudes shown at the Goldsmith's dinner party are those of Sir Aaron Aaronsberg in "The Jewish Trinity." The self-destructive factionalism of the story "Samooborona" has its germ in the satire of *Grandchildren of the Ghetto* (Ch. 9), in which Raphael, as editor of *The Flag of Judah*, witnesses the "members of the Fiddle-de-dee" quarreling with "members of the Fiddle-de-dum," even when both organizations have the same membership. Even Zangwill's "Luftmensch" is in *Children of the Ghetto*, in the *Shalotten Shammos*, the letter writer for the ghetto. Melchitsedek Pinchas, the poet of *Children of the Ghetto*, is central in "The Yiddish *Hamlet*," and Sugarman the Shadchan, also from *Children of the Ghetto*, reappears in the background of several stories.

As we read these stories, we are increasingly aware of the fact that we are reading a single story—one work in which physically scattered people live in one world, united in character and mutual suffering. The effect of coherence in the stories does not depend solely on reference to mutual characters and incidents. The coherence derives also from Zangwill's accumulative portrayal of the complexity of Jewish character—its capacity for love, sacrifice, suffering, and, at times, guile. And it derives from the repeated exploration of the nature of Jews in a Gentile world, where values disintegrate in spite of the force and appeal of tradition and unity.

## CHAPTER 5

# Zangwill's Plays Pleasant and Unpleasant

C ritics generally have been unimpressed by Zangwill's drama, and perhaps a final estimate of his drama demands an adverse critical judgment. At its worst, Zangwill's drama contains melodramatic scenes, stock characters, awkward dialogue, and inflated diction. But at its best, it is a serious and often forceful treatment of important themes. Concerning Zangwill's themes, a recent commentator about Zangwill says, "All this is dead as mutton today." [1] But Zangwill's dramatic themes are as topical today as they were when Zangwill wrote them: the conflicting values of youth and age, the problems of war and peace, the effect of bigotry, the problem of racial assimilation, the fact of religious fanaticism and pious hypocrisy, or the failure of state socialism are topics still worthy of dramatic exploration.

Zangwill, who devoted many years to writing drama, achieved some reputation and popularity as a dramatist. A large part of Zangwill's early drama consists of adaptations of his own short stories and novels: *Children of the Ghetto* (produced in New York and London, 1899), *The Serio-Comic Governess* (produced in New York, 1904), *The King of Schnorrers* (produced in Yiddish in New York, 1905), *The Mantle of Elijah,* and *Merely Mary Ann* (produced in New York, 1904). With the exception of *Merely Mary Ann,* these plays were never published. Also unpublished were a number of other early Zangwill plays: *The Revolted Daughter* (produced in London, 1901), a three-act comedy; *Jinny the Carrier* (produced in Boston, 1905), from which Zangwill later wrote the novel *Jinny the Carrier* (1919); and *Nurse Marjorie* (produced in New York, 1906). His earliest dramas were two curtain raisers: *The Great Demonstration,* written in collaboration with Louis Cowen, produced (1892) in London at the Royal Theatre, and *Six Persons,* also produced in London in 1892 at the Haymarket Theater. [2]

## I   Merely Mary Ann

Zangwill's first notable success in the theatre came in 1904 with a dramatization of his short story "Merely Mary Ann" (1893). It is undoubtedly Zangwill's least artistic major play, but it brought Zangwill "more money than all the ghetto books put together." [3] During the 1904 New York season, it had more than one hundred performances[4] and was later produced in London, in Vienna, and on film three times.[5] The plot of *Merely Mary Ann*—in both the short story and the play—concerns a sensitive and somewhat priggish young artist's increasing love for a lovely, simple serving girl. The dangers of sentimentalism and over-simplification inherent in such a plot Zangwill avoids in the short story by focusing on a secondary conflict—the temptation of the poor artist to prostitute his musical genius by writing songs for the popular market—and by having the lovers part at the end of the story; in the play, Zangwill either could not, or did not, avoid the dangers.

The faults of the play are painfully obvious when it is compared to the short story. The story is divided into three sections, which furnish the essential matter for three acts of the play. In the first section, the musician Lancelot is repelled by but at the same time attracted to Mary Ann, a servant at his roominghouse, who impresses him unfavorably with her rough hands, her dullness, and her naïveté. In the second section, he becomes more and more intrigued with Mary Ann; her country speech is less objectionable to him than cockney and her work-worn hands can be hidden by gloves. Finally, unable to publish his serious work and impelled by poverty and his growing love for Mary Ann, he decides to seek mundane work, leave the roominghouse, and live with Mary Ann. Part III strains our credulity: Mary Ann inherits a fortune from her wandering brother, who has strayed to America, struck oil, and left Mary Ann his heiress at his death. Lancelot overcomes the temptation to marry Mary Ann now that she has money, assures her that she is too good for him, kisses her good-bye, and returns to his work of writing serious music. Mary Ann returns the gloves that Lancelot gave her and goes away, leaving to him her canary, whose joyous song has throughout punctuated their love story.

The play follows the story more or less faithfully for three acts, though it introduces many more characters, most of them dispensable, including a stage Irishman, a stage German, a messenger boy, a drunken medical student, two music-hall dancers, and the Reverend Samuel Smedge. The ironies in the story are made more obvious in the play, as when Lancelot in Act I tells his friend that he shudders at the vulgarity of his brother's marrying an American heiress "whose father has struck ile." [6] Furthermore, Mary's Ann's simplicity, represented in the story as at times charming but more often obtuse, becomes in the play irritatingly "cute," as when Lancelot says, "Oh, dear, am I not an ass!" and Mary Ann replies, "You can't help it, sir. You're so clever" (28). Finally, while the story relies on a rather subtle presentation of the pain attending the love of the mismatched pair, the drama exploits the melodramatic and sentimental possibilities of the story. The story ends as Lancelot resolves, after Mary Ann's departure, to keep the canary "for her"; Act III of the play ends as Mary Ann says good-bye to the bird, as she *"Falls against cage in a passion of tears"* (60).

The major difference between the two works lies in Act IV of the play, an act which has no basis at all in the story except a hint that Lancelot and Mary Ann *might* change. Act IV takes place six years after Act III in the drawing room of a country manor; and Mary Ann (now called Marian) is Lady Chelmer's ward. Marian has undergone a transformation appropriate to her change in status and name: she is witty, self-assured, coy, and clever; she has, she says, lost her innocence and faith, which, like her little canary, died of old age—for "One cannot live in a world like this and keep one's illusions" (81). Nevertheless, she is able to recapture her old self in the final scene, when Lancelot, now a famous composer, returns for her; as he plays the piano, she enters "in her old cap and apron" (which she has conveniently saved for such an occasion?) to be reunited with her lover as "merely Mary Ann."

The play does contain some successful dramatic effects; but most of them are obscured by sentimental excesses. The canary, a symbol of the beauty of Mary Ann's simplicity, is all that Lancelot has left of Mary Ann at the end of the story; in the play, Lancelot has at the end Mary Ann herself, and the canary, like Mary Ann's simplicity, is dead. A final example of the difference between the story and the play is the treatment of

Lancelot's popular song, "Good-night and Good-bye," which he has written for money. In the story, he abhors this song; and, when Mary Ann confesses it is her favorite of all his music, she reveals to him and to us her plebeian tastes. In the play, Lancelot's popular song is theme music for the love story; and Lancelot plays it at the end of Act IV as Mary Ann enters in her old serving girl costume; the curtain falls as the orchestra plays it, *"strings and reeds only."*

## II  The Melting Pot

The dramatic weaknesses of *Merely Mary Ann* Zangwill was not always able to avoid in his future work, but his late drama always escapes superficiality of theme. In fact, the seriousness of theme of Zangwill's most famous drama, *The Melting Pot,* brought him severe criticism from many sides: from Jews horrified by Zangwill's thesis of race assimilation, from equally horrified Christians, from drama critics opposed to the theatrically passionate declamation of the thesis. The criticism of the play was not all hostile, however; it ranged from Theodore Roosevelt's "That's a great play, Mr. Zangwill" at the opening-night performance, to a condemnation of *The Melting Pot* as "Irish stew." [7] The impact of the play is evident from the fact that today people who have never heard of Zangwill have as a part of their everyday vocabulary the phrase he made famous. The play was first performed in Washington, D.C., on October 5, 1908; it then played for a season in Chicago and in New York in 1909. The enthusiasm of American audiences (though not all American drama critics) was not shared by the London theater world when the play was produced in London (1914). "Romantic claptrap," the *Times* critic, A. B. Walkley, called it.[8]

A modern reader of *The Melting Pot* feels vaguely embarrassed by the sentiments expressed in extravagantly rapturous speeches in the play. The play seems dated, and the hero's enthusiasm for America as "God's crucible" seems, if I may use a dated term, "corny." But to say that the play is out of date because Zangwill's dream for America has not been realized is to criticize society's failure, not Zangwill's. Therefore, if we are to judge the play fairly, it should be on its merits as a drama, not on its failure to anticipate the extent of modern cynicism and the long-lived force of prejudice and intolerance.

The play, in four acts, explores the range and results of racial hatred. The plot focuses on the love of a young musician, David Quixano, a Russian-Jewish immigrant to America, and a Russian-Christian immigrant, Vera Revendal. The first act, set in the Quixano living room in New York, introduces Frau Quixano, an Orthodox Jew, who is distressed by the declining faith of her nephew and son, and Mendel Quixano, a pianist turned piano teacher, who cynically predicts for the new immigrant a fate like his—"a terrible struggle for life" resulting in loss of hope and ambition. In contrast to the lonely and bitter elder Quixanos is David, a pogrom orphan who has escaped the Old World and its atrocities (he witnessed the slaughter of his family at Kishineff) to come to America; David wishes to express in his music the spirit of America, "the great Melting-Pot where all the races of Europe are melting and re-forming" into a greater mankind, "perhaps the coming superman." [9]

In Act II, David and Vera fall in love, to the horror of David's Uncle Mendel, who turns his nephew out of the house for having "cast off the God of our fathers" (98). In Act III occurs the scene that one critic termed "theatrically inevitable and inevitably theatrical" [10]: David meets Vera's father, Baron Revendal, and discovers that he is the murderer of innocents at Kishineff, the man in charge when David's family was killed. Though Vera, on learning this terrible truth, rejects Christianity and embraces David's faith, David shrinks from "the butcher's daughter" (158). The act ends as Vera curses her father, the Baron offers to let David kill him, and David refuses this "irrelevance."

In Act IV, which takes place on the roof garden of the settlement house where Vera works, David's American symphony has been performed; but David is unhappy because he, in rejecting Vera, has failed to live up to his dream. He tells Vera: "I preached of God's Crucible, this great new continent that could melt up all race-differences and vendettas, that could purge and re-create, and God tried me with his supremest test. . . . And I said, 'Even thy Crucible cannot melt this hate, cannot drink up this blood!'" (179). Vera's forgiveness comes with her decision to leave him to his music and his dreams, but David begs her to let their love triumph over death; and, as the curtain falls, they look out over New York, hand in hand, proclaiming that "East and West, and North and South, the palm and the pine, the pole and the equator, the crescent and the cross. . . . Here shall . . .

all unite to build the Republic of Man and the Kingdom of God" (184–85).

The theme of the power of love to build a Kingdom of God on earth is presented primarily through the love story of David and Vera. Vera has to overcome anti-Semitic feelings when she first calls on David; but she overcomes her prejudice in her love for David, so much so that she faces the opposition of her outraged father, explaining, "Surely, father, all religions must serve the same God—since there is only one God to serve" (124). David has to overcome an even greater hatred than that of race: in Act III, he rejects Vera because "There is a river of blood between us" (155). But finally he begs forgiveness from the guiltless daughter of his most hated enemy.

The love which unites all races is not a romantic but a spiritual love. Vera's kisses to David at the end of the play are "as we Russians kiss at Easter—the three kisses of peace," and they are given *"in ritual solemnity"* (183). In keeping with the religious theme, Act II, in which David and Vera discover their love, takes place at *Purim,* the Jewish holiday celebrating the salvation of the Jews from massacre and their elevation to favor through the influence of Queen Esther; the story of Esther is, significantly for Zangwill's theme, an intermarriage story. *The Melting Pot* ends on a Saturday, July 4, a holy day (*Shabbos*) of independence.

Other conversions from prejudice to love take place in the play: Kathleen, the Irish servant of the Quixanos, is at first irritated at having to keep a kosher house and at Frau Quixano's Yiddish. But, when David tells Kathleen of Frau Quixano's loneliness and helplessness at separation from her people, Kathleen's intolerance changes to compassion and protective care, so that in Act II Kathleen scolds the Quixano men for not observing *Purim,* refers to "our Passover," and "Proudly" explains to Davenport that she wears a comic false nose to celebrate *Purim* "Bekaz we're Hebrews!" (72)[11] Even Frau Quixano violates her rigid orthodoxy enough to come hear David's concert on the Sabbath, reasoning that David has always played the violin on the Sabbath and that "If the Lord has stood it all these years, He must consider you an exception" (166). So too does Mendel Quixano change his mind about the marriage of Vera and David; like Frau Quixano, he admits that geniuses are probably exceptions to the usual rule, and, besides, "I'd rather see you marry her than go about [in gloom] like this" (165).

The forces of unchanging intolerance are represented in the play by the Revendals—a Russian baron and his aristocratic French wife—and Quincy Davenport, a millionaire American cultivating European ways. To counter these examples of Old World failure are the new Americans: a Russian Christian (Vera), Russian Jews (the Quixanos, especially David), an Irish servant (Kathleen), and a German musician (Herr Pappelmeister). This counterpointing of characters illustrating the forces of prejudice and love could still, no doubt, rouse an audience to an increased concern for the brotherhood of man.

This is not to say that the play does not have faults: it has all the dramatic weaknesses of *Merely Mary Ann*. It has the stage Irishman (here, Irish girl) and the stage German; its climax depends on the coincidence which no amount of foreshadowing (and there is some) can make us believe; and David's impassioned rhetoric leaves us somewhat unconvinced. Furthermore, the play is more "Jewish" than the theme will bear; that is, in a play advocating the assimilation of all races and creeds, Zangwill seems impelled—possibly unconsciously—to slant the statement to favor the Jews. The Christians in the play are for the most part a bad sort: Baron Revendal, constantly invoking Holy Church and Holy Russia, is a monster; his wife the baroness is so intolerant that she refuses even to meet David. The two "good" Christians in the play—Kathleen and Vera—adopt Jewish ways: Kathleen participates in the *Purim* festival, keeps a kosher household, and refers to herself as "Hebrew"; Vera converts to Judaism. Though the Jews in the play are prejudiced, they do no harm; unlike the Christians, Frau and Mendel Quixano's orthodoxy has a quality of tolerance; and, though David hates Vera for her father's sins, he is given such a powerful motive for this hatred—the atrocities committed by Revendal—that we would expect only a superhuman not to behave as David does.

Finally, we detect in the play a note of desperation: it is a dramatization more of Zangwill's hope than of his conviction. In his 1914 afterword to the play, he writes, "To suppose that America will remain permanently afflicted by all the old European diseases would be to despair of humanity, not to mention superhumanity" (204). The play was an alternative to despair. Zangwill was perfectly aware of the potential failure of America to realize his dream; Quincy Davenport is the only native-born American in the play; and he is, David notes, "killing my America"

(86). Nevertheless, the play remains an eloquent, even if somewhat strained, expression of turn-of-the-century idealism.

## III   The War God

*The War God* was produced in London in 1911 at His Majesty's Theater by Sir Herbert Beerbohm Tree; and, though estimates of the dramatic value of the play varied, the critics agreed that the theme of the play merited praise. The theme grows out of the conflict between two powers: pacifism, represented by Count Frithiof, versus power politics, represented by Chancellor Torgrim. Torgrim, a worshiper of the war god, aspires to rule the world and, as chancellor, is the real power in the kingdom of Gothia. When Gothia stops a war with Hunland because of the marriage of Gothia's king and a Hunland princess, Torgrim plans war on Alba; he also plans to have his soldier son succeed to highest military command. He justifies Gothia's militarism with the explanation that "To safeguard peace we must prepare for war," a maxim Frithiof says "was forged in hell." [12]

Frithiof is Torgrim's greatest enemy and the major threat to his power. Frithiof and Torgrim are generally taken—at Zangwill's suggestion—to be based on Tolstoy and Bismarck, respectively; but such identification is not essential; in fact, it is only incidental to understanding the play. Torgrim clearly represents ruthless and ambitious political absolutism in the service of vested money interests, and Frithiof just as clearly represents non-violence and love. As prophet of love and peace, Frithiof is more closely identified with Christ than with Tolstoy. His first words in the play echo Christ's: "What shall it profit a race to gain the world/And lose its soul?" (39) His name, he explains, means "maker of peace"; he says that he "came in love to bring you peace" (40). At the end of Act I Torgrim strikes Frithiof with a glove, after which *"The* COUNT *silently turns the other cheek and stands with calm eyes of love"* (41).

When Osric, Torgrim's son, hears that Frithiof has stopped the revolution, he exclaims, "So Frithiof is our saviour!" (75); and, when the king receives Frithiof over the protests of the courtiers, the king asks, "Has he not bled for me?" to which Frithiof answers, "Not for you, King, but for the famished mob" (77). Frithiof is not, as the revolutionists believe, a supporter of Torgrim; though he deplores violence, he sympathizes with the revolutionists' cause and complains that taxes for war are keeping the people in poverty. He diagnoses war as the instrument of capitalism: "The God of War is now a man of business—/With vested interests"; and he predicts no freedom from "this trade in death" as long as "this social order lives" (79-80).

His creed, uttered in Act III as the anarchists threaten his life, consists of these maxims: " 'Judge not lest ye be judged' " (88) and "Who takes the sword shall perish with the sword" (95). He urges inner, spiritual reform as a first stage to social reform; killing the "Blind instruments of blinder social systems" will do no good, he argues. At his death the parallels to Christ's passion are unmistakable: to Norna's cry of "Death" to him, he says, "I pity you— you know not what you do"; he knows that his spirit ("of universal love") cannot be killed (97-99). When Brog fires at Frithiof, "FRITHIOF *stands serenely as before*," and Brog swears, "Christ!" When Norna finally shoots Frithiof, his dying words are "Peace! / Only my body dies: my spirit is with you/Always . . ." (105).

A third power in the play is represented by Comrade Brog, the leader of the anarchists; by Norna, the heroine of the play; and by Baron Konrad, a spy at court. The purpose of the anarchists is to topple the government commanded by Torgrim, whose wars are destroying the people; the anarchists' methods Norna states: "Cut off the heads of war and war collapses. . . . So death to statesmen!" (51) They are opposed to Frithiof, for he thwarted Brog's popular revolution by appealing to the force of Christian love and by bidding the people to abandon their weapons. Frithiof's pacifism makes him, they say, a "Governmental tool" who "Has squashed our country's finest chance of freedom" (89). Therefore they destroy Frithiof, and, ironically, become themselves tools of Torgrim's government, for Torgrim wants Frithiof's murder blamed on the anarchists. As he explains, "One single stroke will rid us of the zealot/And turn the vengeance of his followers/ Against our other foes—the anarchists" (82).

Torgrim's control and power are shown symbolically in the setting of the play. Acts I and V, depicting (I) the initiation of Torgrim's plans for war and power and (V) the destruction of Torgrim primarily because of the success of his plans, are set in Torgrim's study. Acts II and IV, depicting (II) the love of Norna and Osric and the failure of Brog's revolution and (IV) the hopelessness of the love of Norna and Osric, are set on a royal castle terrace. Act III, depicting the assassination of Frithiof, is set on "a grassy plateau in the mountains" in the camp of the revolutionaries.

The movement of the action and setting is outward—from the chancellor's study, to the royal terrace, to the anarchists' camp—and then back to the source of all the machinations, the originator of the actions of both the royal family and the anarchists, the chancellor; the setting of the play begins and ends where the action begins and ends—with the chancellor. The central episode, the killing of Frithiof by the anarchists, seems to be free from Torgrim's control, but it was in actuality planned by him. Ironically, Frithiof's assassination destroys Torgrim; for his son, on whom his hopes for the future depend, becomes after Frithiof's death a Frithian. And, when Osric finds that his beloved Norna killed Frithiof, he calls Norna a "sacrilegious murderess" and kills himself, thus destroying the object of Torgrim's ambition and Norna's love. At the end of the play, the worshiper of the war god and the advocate of violence and revenge are left in desolation; but the Frithians outside the chancellor's window chant a hymn to Frithiof, "The Prophet of Love."

The triumph of Frithiof's philosophy of love is demonstrated not only by the conversion of Osric but of an anarchist, Konrad, who, after witnessing Frithiof's death, sobs "Master!" Even the chancellor's confidential secretary, Karl Blum, becomes a Frithian. Blum is especially interesting as another of Zangwill's examples of a Christianized Jew. Blum makes the arrangements for putting into effect Torgrim's plots and has so much power that he tells Torgrim that "*You* ruled his Majesty,/And *I* ruled you, and so the Ghetto-brat/Has been the sovereign of Gothia" (148). Blum has been baptized a Christian; but, when Torgrim, enraged, calls him "a dirty Jew," Blum admits that he was never really Christian, that he "knew your weakness for converting Jews,/So played upon it" (145).

In this play, as in his other writings, Zangwill makes a distinction between Holy Church and true Christianity. The first, represented by Revendal in *The Melting Pot* and Torgrim in *The War God,* is identified with hatred, persecution, and violence; the second stands for love, tolerance, and pacifism, as do the Frithians in *The War God.* Blum makes the distinction for Torgrim, saying

We Jews, who bidden rise *beyond* the code
Of eye for eye, must rub both eyes to see
Not e'en eye-justice done in Christendom,
Whose cannons thunder 'gainst both God and Christ. (146)

Thus Blum does not become Christian, for the Christians hate Jews and wage war; but he does become Frithian—a practicer of true Christianity. Finally, then, in the struggle for power, Frithiof wins. In Act II, Frithiof tells Torgrim, "Brog, you and I—we three —contest the world/. . . . Brog lawless, you with law, or I with love" (80). Though Frithiof dies, his followers believe in his resurrection and ascension (130); and certainly the spirit of brotherhood, love, and peace lives at the end of *The War God*.

## IV  *Two Plays about Religion*

Zangwill's next play, *The Next Religion* (1912), shifts from a predominantly political theme to a religious one. Its subject proved too bold, however, for the Lord Chamberlain, the censor of plays, who forbade the performance of the play in Great Britain. The play was no doubt censored because the Lord Chamberlain, like most critics of it, misunderstood its thesis; they erroneously thought Zangwill was an exponent of the Reverend Stephen Trame's new religion in the play. Even a reader as sympathetic to Zangwill as Wohlgelernter assumes that Trame's philosophy is Zangwill's and that the three saints in Trame's temple—Mazzini, Emerson, and Swinburne—are the saints of a Zangwill theology. The theme of *The Next Religion* is not that economic man "must awaken to the memory of the ties that bind them with the rest of mankind," following the ideals of brotherhood, reason, and love preached by Mazzini, Emerson, and Swinburne;[13] this analysis ignores Act III, in which the new religion, capitalist supported, becomes as ritualistic, dogmatic, and superstitious as the religion Trame intended to replace.

The tenets of the new religion are presented in Act I by Reverend Trame, an Anglican minister dissatisfied with traditional religion. Trame's new religion "accepts the Revelation of Science" and worships "the God of Law. The God who will send tuberculosis even through the communion chalice"; this God, made apparent through man's increasing knowledge of the universe, is "infinitely larger than the God of our fathers";[14] He is an impersonal God who cannot be begged through prayer to dole out favors and who does not offer man personal immortality. According to Trame, the holy spirit of God is within man, who must work for social reform and give up the otherworldliness of Christianity. As Trame says, "we might have cleaned out our swamp of misery and evil centuries ago if we hadn't looked to some gigantic genie in the clouds to do all our dirty work and give us golden floors to squat on into the bargain" (33). To bring these truths to man, Trame calls for no formal religion; organization, he argues, corrupts religious ideals; the new religion requires no temple, no paid priesthood, no dogma, only man striving to bring the Kingdom of God—the ideals of "purity, peace, and brotherhood"—on earth (158).

In Act I, Trame reveals to his atheist friend, Hal McFadden, that the only thing keeping Trame in the Anglican priesthood is his wife Mary, the orthodox daughter of an Anglican bishop. He is, however, finally driven to leave the ministry by the uncharitable behavior of his Christian flock: Squire Rowley, a member of Trame's church, evicts tenant-farmer Burr because he is an outspoken atheist; and a blacksmith, Eli Oakshott, quoting Scriptures and wielding a hammer, attacks Burr for his blasphemies. Stephen, who damns Oakshott's theology of wrath and violence, resolves to leave the ministry to preach the new religion. Mary agrees to follow him, for "I took you for better or worse—for wiser or sillier" (74).

Act II finds the Trame family two years later in poverty in Whitechapel, Trame having made only two converts to his new religion: Farmer Burr and the teacher of Trame's son at Board School. When Trame learns that his book, *The Next Religion,* has sold out the first edition, he believes that "Truth will out, even in England" (88); but he discovers that Mary's father, the missionary bishop of Soudan, has purchased the blasphemous and heretical books for a bonfire. When their poverty is most acute and when Mary and Stephen are faced with almost certain starvation, Mary prays for "a redeemer," who appears—too promptly for dramatic probability but in accord with Zangwill's theme—in the person of Sir Thomas McFadden (Hal's father), a millionaire armaments manufacturer who wants to join the new religion and give his millions to its development. Against his better judgment,

Trame yields to Mary's urging and accepts the money, though he knows that McFadden "doesn't understand the next religion one iota" (136).

Act III shows Trame's new religion ten years later: it is thriving on McFadden's money. It has a temple (Saint Thomas's), saints (Thomas McFadden, Mazzini, Emerson, Swinburne); elaborate ritual, hereditary priesthood, and a training college for priests; "decoration and symbolism" (robes, palms, lilies, music, altar); and branches in almost every civilized capital. Trame is preparing to dedicate the new temple with a sermon on true immortality. Hal McFadden, now converted to Anglicanism, points out that Stephen's pomp and ritual are close to Catholicism; that Stephen's followers worship his example of "suffering and self-sacrifice," not truth; and that "To do good without hope of reward makes you even more Christian than the Christians" (166–69). Eli Oakshott enters once again (still wielding a hammer) to destroy the Antichrist, but he destroys Stephen's son instead. The temple service begins, and Stephen asks for "the choir-circuits for the dead" and his son's Requiem. The play ends as Stephen goes out to preach his rationalist sermon; and Mary, cursing the law governing Stephen's universe, turns once again, "ecstatically transfigured," to her faith in "The Resurrection and the Life!" (193)

The play is a dramatic study of types of religious fanaticism. Eli Oakshott, violent, self-righteous, and cruel, represents a vindictive, vengeful, intolerant religion—the Christianity of *The War God;* Squire Rowley is a milder version of the same viciousness and intolerance. The bishop of the Soudan represents unthinking Christianity, obedience to the forms of an established religion. Mary Trame also represents unthinking piety, but she is above all maternal. Because her son is a member of the new religion, she too is converted, reasoning, "If the heart of *youth* goes towards this religion, then surely this religion is blessed of God to be the next religion, and we that are old and set must cast off our prejudices" (156). But when her son is killed, she is emotionally incapable of accepting Stephen's faith and returns to her concept of a heaven in which she and her dead son, "eternally eighteen," will be reunited.

Finally, Stephen Trame himself represents a truly religious impulse striving to express itself in a new form but failing because of, first, a failure to take into account man's irrationality and emotionality and, second, a mistaken notion that the armament manufacturer's money will spread the new religion. At the end of the play, Stephen is as fanatic as the others about the rightness of his religion and the sincerity of his form of worship; his fetishism and superstition are apparent as he calls for a sheaf of electric cables, so that "I can finger them as I preach—my pores can suck in their electric stimulus" (151).

Stephen Trame is, then, far from a spokesman for Zangwill; he is Zangwill's dramatization of the futility of striving for a new religion. The man who comes closest to expressing Zangwill's values in the play is Hal McFadden, the atheist converted by love and fatherhood to Christianity (to true Christianity, not Oakshott's kind); Hal argues:

HAL: What have you found more beautiful or uplifting than the words of Christ? And this religion has the advantage of being already organized—it carries the inspiration and consecration of the centuries.

STEPHEN: And their encrustation of error! And their petrifactions!

HAL: Then vivify it, scour it, bring it back to the Founder. Perhaps Christ's own religion has never had a chance—perhaps *that's* the next religion. (165–66)

The statement is a familiar one in Zangwill's drama: Christianity as Christ preached it (as Frithiof preaches it in *The War God*)— a religion of peace, brotherhood, and love, a religion not yet come to the earth—is the way toward the Kingdom of God.

Stephen Trame, whose new religion too quickly takes on the perversions of an old religion, would seem Zangwill's answer to late Victorian and Edwardian advocates of a modern religion to replace the worn-out creeds inherited from the past. "Creeds must become intellectually honest," Bernard Shaw had said in his Preface (1906) to *Major Barbara*. "At present there is not a single credible established religion in the world." [15] I quote from Shaw's Preface to *Major Barbara* because parallels in character, setting, and ideology suggest that *The Next Religion* is Zangwill's specific reply to *Major Barbara*.[16] Barbara, the heroine of Shaw's play, has rejected the Anglicanism of her mother for the Christianity of the Salvation Army; but, when she discovers that it depends on contributions from corrupt sources, she abandons it. Finally, she is converted to the revolutionary (and evolutionary) religion of her father, Andrew Undershaft, a millionaire munitions manufacturer and one of the sources of support for the Salvation Army. In the final act, Undershaft (called by Shaw St. Andrew Undershaft) takes Barbara through his munitions factory, which includes a model village for the well-cared-for workers, with churches for the villagers; he advises her,

Well, you have made for yourself something that you call a morality or a religion or what not. It doesnt fit the facts. Well, scrap it. Scrap it and get one that does fit. That is what is wrong with the world at present. It scraps its obsolete steam engines and dynamos; but it wont scrap its old prejudices and its old moralities and its old religions and its old political constitutions. Whats the result? In machinery it does very well; but in morals and religion and politics it is working at a loss that brings it nearer bankruptcy every year. Dont persist in that folly. If your old religion broke down yesterday, get a newer and a better one for tomorrow.[17]

Barbara gives up, as Stephen Trame does, "the bribe of heaven," the belief in immortality, to work for the Kingdom of God on earth. Trame's religion includes other aspects of Shaw's religion of the Life Force, for example, the ideas that "The same Holy Ghost is in us all" and that God is "an eternal weaving and unweaving" (*The Next Religion,* 18, 191).

The perversion of Trame's religion in Zangwill's play suggests that the money of a wealthy munitions manufacturer (St. Thomas McFadden or St. Andrew Undershaft) is the last thing needed to make creeds honest. McFadden's money buys temples and robes and founds schools; it makes a formalized religion—which both Zangwill and Shaw distrusted—of an ideal of peace and brotherhood. To make his point about the failure of McFadden/Undershaft money to change man, Zangwill modifies Shaw's cannon maker so that he is recognizable only by his profession; in place of the philosophic Undershaft is the merely iconoclastic McFadden, who hates Christians and confuses temple-building with religion-founding. And Zangwill's McFadden, coming as an answer to Mary's prayer, serves as confirmation of Mary's God, who apparently exists but not in so simple a form as Mary imagines: the redeemer whom He sends saves the Trames from starvation but wrecks Trame's religion.

The failure of Trame's religion is seen symbolically in Zangwill's treatment of a fertility theme. Act I, set at harvest time, introduces Wilfred, Trame's son, whom Trame regards as his only immortality; for the boy is Trame's only child, and Mary can have no more children. The curtain falls on Act I as Mary is typing Trame's harvest sermon on the text, "That Thou givest them they gather: Thou openest Thine hand, they are filled with good" (74). Trame's hope is, he says in Act II, that *The Next Religion* will cause seeds to flower: "They will germinate. Do you realise, Mary, the power of a little seed? To undermine buildings, to throw off the weight of earth, to shoot up living branches towards the sky?" (123)

However, the snow falling throughout Act II (set in November) suggests the real fate of Trame's new religion. Act III shows the blossoms, already dying and soon dead, of Trame's new religion; Trame believes that "Everywhere the old thought decays and dies, and new is burgeoning and blossoming" (151); but Wilfred, his only son, is cut down. Since Trame believes that a man's immortality rests in his children, his final sermon on true immortality becomes a meaningless ritual after his son's death.

The reason for Trame's fruitless harvest is suggested symbolically by his steadily failing vision. In Act I, his sight is bad enough to require medicine; in Act II, it is failing; and, in Act III, it has— as has his religion—totally failed. Trame is blind, though called by his disciples both "Master" and "Seer." Trame believes that his blindness allows him to see "only the souls" of his disciples; but Hal says that his blindness served as "a sensation," made him "a sort of martyr," and brought more converts than either Trame's eloquence or McFadden's money. Finally, after the death of Wilfred, Mary accuses Trame of spiritual blindness and forbids him "to infect others with your blindness . . . to make this dark world darker" (193).

Zangwill continued to explore a religious subject in his next play, *Plaster Saints,* which was produced at the Comedy Theater (London) in 1914. This play has as its theme the hypocrisy necessary when society expects perfection of human beings. Dr. Rodney Vaughan, a Protestant clergyman, is concealing a secret sin—a love affair with his secretary, Felicia Morrow, who has left him and given birth to his child. In Act I of the play, Reverend Vaughan's wife, Hannah, discovers that, because of Felicia's disgrace, Felicia's brother Hubert cannot marry the daughter of a respectable churchman, Sir John Archmundham. As Hannah searches for evidence to convince Sir John that he should allow the marriage of his daughter and Hubert, she discovers that her husband is the father of Felicia's baby.

How the clergyman and his pious wife work out the problem of living with Dr. Vaughan's sin constitutes the major action of the play. When Hannah overcomes her shock and revulsion at her husband's guilt, she argues that a clean confession is the only way to live honestly. Dr. Vaughan at first disagrees, for he wishes to continue God's work; he argues that his sin and repentance have made him a more sympathetic man and a better minister. But he is persuaded by Hannah to confess publicly and, as he says, "sweep away this modern cant of the plaster priest!" and build a "church of reality." [18] Then Hannah changes her mind when her daughter becomes engaged to Sir John's son; in order for her daughter to marry the man she loves, Hannah and Dr. Vaughan remain silent. Vaughan resigns his curacy and resolves to continue to crusade for moral causes "not with the saintliness of the priest" but "as a man among men" (210).

The theme of the play is developed in the symbol of plaster saints; these saints are like the hypocrites compared in the New Testament to "whited sepulchres, which indeed appear beautiful outward, but are within full of dead men's bones, and of all uncleanness," and who "outwardly appear righteous unto men, but within . . . are full of hypocrisy and iniquity." [19] In the play, the image of the "whited sepulchre" reinforces that of the plaster saint. For example, when Sir John discovers that Dr. Vaughan, troubled by insomnia, sleeps in the study, he says of the pillow cases hidden beneath the divan cushions: "Whited sepulchres! Who would think anything in *your* house ever led a double life?" (29). When Hannah discovers the truth about her husband, she exclaims, "You can't go on preaching while you yourself are a whited sepulchre" (167). In the final scene, Dr. Vaughan is protesting the idea of clergymen as "a collection of plaster saints" (212).

The hypocrisy is made necessary by the unforgiving Puritanism of Sir John, who believes that "the sinner shall be cut off root and branch" (69). He also believes that the sins of the fathers should be visited on the children or, to be strictly accurate, that Felicia's sin makes her brother unworthy of Sir John's daughter: "Tainted stock is tainted stock," says Sir John (190). He is supported in this belief by his scientist son, John, who has given up practice as a doctor to study the working of Mendel's law. Ironically, Sir John is delighted with his son's marriage to Elsie, Vaughan's daughter; but he is distressed at Amy's marriage to Felicia Morrow's brother. Finally, the women—Hannah, Amy, and Elsie—defy the idea of "tainted stock," insisting that people are not "like potatoes" (192). They are, as Dr. Vaughan and Hannah know, to their sorrow, infinitely more complex.

The play succeeds in its examination of a serious problem but fails as a whole because of its uneven tone. Its subtitle, *A High Comedy in Three Movements,* suggests a major reason for its failure. The three movements of the play present, amplify, and resolve the major theme of guilt and hypocrisy. But this theme is accompanied by a minor theme of the conflict of generations, and in treating this conflict as "a high comedy," Zangwill directs our attention away from the serious major theme. The arch dialogue, the "cleverness" of the young people, and the comic resolution of all their problems in a double marriage are not in keeping with the tone of the major struggle.

## V  Too Much Money

In Zangwill's next play, written during World War I and performed at the Ambassadors Theater (London) in 1918, Zangwill turned to comedy. *Too Much Money,* he says in an author's note to the play, was written as a release from "the tragic tension" of the war.[20] The setting is prewar; Act I takes place in the rich Mayfair drawing room of Annabel and Thomas Broadley, who have "too much money." Broadley, "a born millionaire," has a wife who despises her husband's vulgarity and his riches. To relieve her boredom, she has determined to study "life-enhancing" art, lavishing money on Grandison Tiptree, "a Futurist painter," and his fiancée, Thisbe Leach, whose character is described by her name. Broadley decides to bring his wife to her senses by following the advice of a self-made millionaire, Sir Robert McCorbel, and pretending to be bankrupt.

Act II, "a fortnight later," finds the Broadleys in a garret, where Annabel is thriving on "life-enhancing" poverty and her husband is suffering from bad food, inferior cigars, and dreadful living quarters. Farcical action—including Annabel's burning up her husband's pajamas with a hot iron and dumping water out the window on a woman's head—dominates the scene, which rises to a climax after the landlady, noticing the presence of too much money in an apartment of presumed paupers, becomes convinced that they are counterfeiters and calls the police. But Miss Roseleaf, Broadley's former housekeeper (who is secretly conducting his financial affairs), identifies them and saves them from jail. The act ends as Sir Robert announces that Annabel's foolish investment of five pounds in the cheapest stock on the market has made her forty pounds; she excitedly tells Broadley that she has found the way to restore their fortunes "At the real place to coin money— the Stock Exchange!" (73)

Act III returns to the Broadley's Mayfair drawing room the following April, where Annabel is absorbed in the problems of high finance. Annabel now reads nothing but stock exchange lists, and she is interested in Tiptree's paintings only as speculative ventures. Miss Roseleaf explains that Annabel "has become one of the greatest and most daring operators in London, that in one short year she has turned a five-pound note into a colossal fortune" (76). When Broadley, maddened by his wife's scorn of him, confesses his hoax to Annabel, she immediately begins planning how they can invest his money.

In the play, money is the reason for the follies or vices of all the characters; it is responsible for Annabel's art-craze and her speculative-craze, for her husband's ineptness, for Sir Robert's arrogance, for Tiptree's and Leach's schemes to extort money from Annabel. The refrain of "too much money" runs through Act I, accounting for Annabel's boredom with her life and her husband. In Act II, the Broadleys have moved to a pauper's dwelling because their former lodgings cost "too much money" (42); Annabel refuses to give Miss Roseleaf a testimonial because, when she was their housekeeper, she "spent too much money" (54); finally, Broadley is arrested because the landlady "saw too much money" (60). In Act III, the refrain continues to the end of the play, where Annabel seriously explains to her husband that "for these great operations [her financial dealings] one can't have TOO MUCH MONEY" (102).

In addition to the obvious theme of the corrupting power of

money, Zangwill also explores a Feminist theme. Zangwill's women in this play are in control of their men, of their homes, and even of the society. For example, Miss Lilian Roseleaf, as her name suggests, is "an exquisitely pretty and petite Puritan figure, the apparent quintessence of early Victorian girlishness"; but she is in reality "a supremely efficient modern scientific housekeeper and a celebrated suffragist speaker" (2). She keeps Broadley's affairs in order and supports her playwright husband. Annabel, though she protests that "gowns and gawds" are "the badge of serfdom," dominates her husband; and, in Act III, she becomes even legal master (the owner) of their home. She talks baby talk to her husband and is convinced that not he nor any man can manage money.

The movement of the play is cyclic: the play begins and ends in April in the Broadley drawing room. The comic figures suffer no change in character; they are not, to use a Jonsonian phrase, brought out of their "humours." Annabel simply exchanges one "humour" (playing the stock market, Act III) for another (affecting a passion for art, Act I, or for work, Act II). Nor is Thomas Broadley changed: he is dominated throughout by his wife. Zangwill conceived of his play as farce with "a background of contemporary satire and portraiture" (Author's Note, v); but, because of its comic and satiric force, the play is probably best described as a satirical comedy with farcical elements.

## VI  *Two Plays about Politics*

Zangwill returned to the serious pacifist and antinationalist themes of *The War God* in his next play, *The Cockpit* (1921). In this play Queen Marguerita of Valdania has been reared in New York as the daughter of a self-exiled Balkan chancellor, Nicholas Stone, who escaped the political quarrels destroying Europe to start life anew in America. Stone, who has written a book called *The Nemesis of Nationality,* hates Europe, which he considers "a pit of steel-spurred cocks each crowing on its own little dunghill." [21] But a Valdanian general and marquis discover him and Marguerita and demand that they return to Valdania to prevent revolution. Stone refuses and begs the queen to do the same, but she feels a call to serve her country. Acts II and III depict the disillusionment of the young queen, whose reform measures are ignored and whose idealism fails to make any impression on the war-mongers, the politically ambitious, and the vacillating populace. At the end of the play, war is about to break out, the domestic affairs of Valdania are still in need of reform, and the Queen has barely missed a hateful political marriage. She came to Valdania to usher in an era of peace and love but finds herself "Queen in a Cockpit" instead.

In Valdania, the clergy, the capitalists, and the statesmen use the queen to promote their nationalistic ambitions; and the queen's efforts for peace are perverted by the machinations of her military and political advisors. General Roxo and the Marquis Fiuma, who discovered the queen and brought her back to Valdania, note that her return from long exile has renewed the war fever of Valdanians, who "toast her by her obsolete title of 'Duchess of Bosnavina' and . . . would die for her to a man" (86). The first result of the queen's return is, then, that Valdania wages war to annex Bosnavina. So too, when the queen's peaceful and loving nature converts her political rival, Marrobio, to allegiance to her, this conversion is turned to military advantage; for Marrobio leads Valdanian forces to victory in Bosnavina.

Her realm is also torn by internal strife. Stone outlines the religious scene of Valdania: Roman Catholics, Greek Orthodox, and Moslems all hate one another: "The only thing the three religions had in common except Jew-baiting was the hatred of a neighbor State" (34). During the time of the play all religions are united in a war against Bosnavina; the Moslem, Marrobio, leads an army into battle; the Catholic cardinal and the Orthodox patriarch "blessed the banners" and "turned church-bells into cannon"; and a Jew (converted to Catholicism) finances the war. As in *The War God,* Holy Church supports nationalism and war instead of peace and the brotherhood of man; it condones lies and a loveless, even "loathsome," marriage for the queen. Baron Gripstein, a Christianized Jew, is described by Chancellor Cazotti as being "as fervent a Catholic as you, and an even fiercer Anti-Semite" (114). Like his dramatic predecessor, Karl Blum in *The War God,* he is hated by the Christians, who resent his wearing "the Order of the Redeemer" and who, when the war goes badly, blame the Jews and burn the Jewish quarter of the city.

The queen is gradually educated to the nature of European politics. In Act III, she is completely controlled by corrupt forces outside herself. Angered by the lack of success in the war, the same populace that worshiped the queen in Act II now cries for her death, only to be swayed to praise once more at the news of Marrobio's victory. The queen finally realizes that her people are a "mob, mindless as the sea in its smiles and furies" (258); she knows that the clergy and statesmen are ready to sell her in marriage for political power; and she recognizes that war with the province of Rolmenia, whose prince she did not marry, is to follow. Finally, she finds that she cannot escape from the cockpit, for civil war will erupt if another is crowned in Valdania. The curtain falls on a tragic queen in a throne room hung with conquered Bosnavinian flags, as the music of a hymn, "Happy those that fear the Lord," mingles with that of the Valdanian national anthem.

In *The Cockpit,* a pacifist, Vittorio, is persecuted and killed. Zangwill's next play, *The Forcing House, or The Cockpit Continued* (1923), focuses on the triumph of Vittorio's party, a pacifist-Socialist party which replaces Queen Marguerita's rule. Act I of *The Forcing House* has Vittorio's son, Riffoni the Red, confronting the queen, Cazotti, and Baron Gripstein. Riffoni has been in prison for distributing pacifist poems (his father's *Songs of Brotherhood*) during the Bosnavinian war, and now he is to be exiled for his Socialist views. The act ends with Riffoni's vow to return to a Socialist state of Valdania; when Act II begins, one year later, Riffoni, not the queen, is in control of Valdania; and the throne room has become "The People's Hall."

The succeeding acts show that Riffoni's Socialist state is simply the old tyranny with a new name. Though the party preaches equality, inequalities exist: Corporal Vanni, who in *The Cockpit* served the monarchy, in *The Forcing House* bullies his men and his former officer; Salaret, the editor of the party paper, the *Sera,* is a state leader with all the privileges and vices of the former aristocracy. Though the party is pacifist, the Valdanian army is at war with Rolmenia; to protect "the Workers' Republic—the spiritual hope of the world," new deadly weapons have been invented.[22] Political purges and thought control are a way of life. The new editor of the *Sera* has been shot, crying "Long live liberty!"; the people are forbidden to read anything except party organs; and officers of the state are forced to profess atheism, and the churches have been closed. Economic reform is as far away as in the days of the monarchy: children still starve; supplies are scarce; and the state buys from capitalistic importers, "speculators and profiteers." In short, Riffoni's experiment is a disaster; and Cazotti, a Machiavellian like Torgrim in *The War God,* becomes at the end the new king of Valdania.

The theme of *The Forcing House* is an extremely pessimistic one: man is not yet ready for self-government, and states will be ruled by political monsters—whether they be Riffoni the Red or Cazotti the power politician. The duke d'Azolla, speaking as a condemned remnant of the old aristocracy, calls the totalitarian socialism of Riffoni "a forcing house": "Socialism while you won't wait. Not a Paradise of blossoming brotherhood, not a natural growth under God's heaven, but a Socialism ripened prematurely under the heat of compulsion and watered with blood: a Socialism under a sky of glass, unstable, sterile, without spontaneous sap, that can be perpetuated only by ever-renewed compulsion" (169). In order to hold the state together, Riffoni resorts to "brute strength," for "Force is all that the West respects—only by ruthlessness can we save our Republic from the foes without and the still more dangerous foes within" (208). Finally realizing, however, that his republic is a moral failure, Riffoni sends Queen Marguerita back to America and then kills himself; he despairs of both "force and love, while our breed remains so poor" (277–78). The play ends with Cazotti in complete power —Marguerita is gone and Riffoni dead; and the crowd yells *"Viva Cazotti!"*

If *The Cockpit* and *The Forcing House* are regarded as a unit, their structure is cyclic: in Act I of *The Cockpit* Marguerita leaves America, determined to save Valdania from internal strife; and in Act IV of *The Forcing House* she returns to America, having failed in her mission. The plays illustrate the failure of two kinds of reform governments: Christian idealism (*The Cockpit*) and socialism (*The Forcing House*). Both plays trace the rise to power of Cazotti, who uses first the queen's Christianity and then Riffoni's socialism as instruments to increase his own power, which thrives on military strength, internal dissension, and political intolerance.

The plays also trace the career of the conscience of Baron Gripstein, whose rejection of Judaism is at a tremendous personal cost. In a moment of sadness for his sons, one killed and another blinded in Bosnavina, he tells Riffoni that "bodily hunger is not so horrible as this gnawing of the heart"; he recalls his childhood in the ghetto, where his family suffered from bodily but not spiritual hunger: "the Sabbath hallowed it with peace. Ah, I have never been so happy since" (*The Forcing House*, 28). Finally, when Gripstein is sentenced to death by the Socialists, he insists that a rabbi, not a priest, hear his confession of sins.

## VII   We Moderns, *The End of a Long Career*

After these political plays, Zangwill ended a long dramatic career as he began it, with comedy. In his last play, *We Moderns* (produced in New York in 1924), he returned to one of his favorite themes: the conflict of generations. The play, attacked by critics for its opposition to modern psychology and art, is a satire on the absurd tendencies in both; but it is an even stronger attack on the failures of the older generation. To the criticism that "There are times . . . when one is baffled to know whether the author sympathizes with the mid-Victorians or the moderns,"[23] we can answer that Zangwill sympathized with neither when either struck him as ridiculous.

Act I introduces the central conflict, Robert Sundale and his wife versus their children, Mary and Dick. The beginning of the play focuses on the failures of the elder Sundales, who are worrying about the servant problem when millions are dying of starvation, whose conservatism will not allow servants or children to read "immoral" books, and whose methods of dealing with the young are fatuous and repressive. Their son, a Cubist painter, has been dismissed at Oxford, which he calls "a dirty medieval monastery"; he tells his father that "We moderns have grown out of your standards, they're too small"; and he blames his father's generation for having "reduced Europe to a shambles . . .—to a bankrupt estate."[24] Their daughter is obsessed with modern theories of psychoanalysis and is an admirer of the "immoral" poet, Oscar Pleat; she refuses to accept a long-term engagement with John Ashlar, D.S.O., but agrees instead to elope with him to his new assignment in Mesopotamia.

In Act II, set in Dick's studio, the dandy and esthete, Oscar Pleat, dominates the action; he often refers to "we moderns" in order to justify his old-fashioned scoundrelism, which includes abandoning his old love, Dolly, and attempting to seduce Mary. Dolly has put into practice the *carpe diem* philosophy which she espouses and, as a result, is now pregnant with Pleat's child. Though she hates the idea of marriage, she agrees to marry Dick when he proposes. Dick then rejects the idea of emancipation from an old morality because of his love for Dolly and his horror at Pleat's desertion of her. And Mary is saved from Pleat's attempted seduction by the arrival of John and her father.

In Act III, the old and young are reconciled, as the Sundale youths give up the worst of their modern ideas and the parents admit that their morality has also failed. Mary agrees to a long-term engagement to John. Her father buys Dick's worst painting to give him money for his marriage, and he comes to realize that "You can't Yale-lock the young generation—we muddled things—with our Great War and our Little Peace—and they know it" (189). Finally, the conflict is resolved in favor of youth, who—if they have been guilty of extravagances in philosophy and behavior—are nevertheless the only hope for the world; Sundale tells his daughter that she must leave her parents behind: "It's only right you should go sunwards, with faith and hope of your own. Only do have a little charity for us as we go down to the dust" (204).

In addition to his examination of the values of old and young, Zangwill also glances at modern art, artists, and art criticism in the play. One of the central characters, Dick, is an artist who uses "subjects or sitters merely to express *Me!*" (23) He is currently painting "a beautiful but somewhat conventional picture" of a mermaid, and he has a gondola painting which a critic calls a "Venetian sonata in B minor." Though Zangwill could hardly approve of Dick's idea of art as merely the expression of the artist's temper, he would approve finally of Dick's rightness of feeling for Dolly and his contempt for Oscar Pleat, the effete artist. And we should note that Zangwill's play, like Dick's painting, is a sonata; specifically, according to the subtitle, it is a comedy "in Three Movements (Allegro, Andante, Adagio)."

Oscar Pleat, the author of *Meditations of a Modern,* who preaches "the gospel of . . . hedonism" in "a mincing Oxford accent," is a refugee from "the yellow nineties"; he is cast in the role of melodramatic villain—the unfaithful lover and seducer of young women. Another artist satirized in the play is Joanna Herzberg, author of *Glad Cucumbers,* "an exercise in the subconscious";

she also writes a newspaper column, which she cynically admits is mostly manufactured. Joanna smokes a pipe, is "massive," and wears an "epicene" costume; she is going to marry for a third time —this time a ruined Royal Academy painter, ruined by "us modern critics" who "boosted all the freak painters and sculptors" and ignored the Academy.

*We Moderns* is hardly an impressive close to Zangwill's career as playwright. In evaluating Zangwill's dramas, we certainly cannot say that Zangwill was a great, or even a consistently good, dramatist. The plays contain too many scenes dominated by "stagey" rhetoric, too many instances of inconsistent tone, too few memorable characters and even fewer really engaging ones. Some of the plays are unquestionably failures: *Merely Mary Ann,* because of its sentimentality and melodramatic clichés; *Plaster Saints,* because of its uneven tone. *The Next Religion,* as an answer to Bernard Shaw's *Major Barbara,* is an interesting and historically important play; but its satire on the new religion is now dated, though its theme—the triumph of religious fanaticism—is not. *We Moderns* is also dated; the esthete and the New Woman are still with us, but not in the form satirized in Zangwill's play.

Zangwill's most famous play, *The Melting Pot,* though not his best, deserves a place in the history of English and American drama as an early, impassioned hope for the triumph of love and brotherhood in the American character. Zangwill's best plays are those constituting a political trilogy: *The War God,* affirming the eventual triumph of love and nonviolence over hatred and war, is Zangwill's expression of what ought to be; *The Cockpit* and *The Forcing House,* realistically facing the failure of modern politics, is Zangwill's pessimistic appraisal of what actually exists. These plays will remain current and meaningful as long as hypocrisy, ambition, intolerance, and violence trouble the world.

## CHAPTER 6

# "Fine Feathers" of Verse

Zangwill, who was not a good poet, wrote and published poems in dozens of magazines and journals;[1] he published a volume of selected poems in 1903; and he wrote a play in blank verse in 1911. But in few of his poems does he achieve the stature of even a good minor poet. Perhaps one critic's recommendation that "the best thing to do with his [Zangwill's] sonnet on Theodore Herzl is to keep it decently out of sight"[2] ought to be applied to all Zangwill's poetry. But, for the sake of thoroughness in examining Zangwill as artist, we should briefly consider his poetry since it makes up a substantial portion of his work. In addition to his original poetry, Zangwill made numerous translations of Hebrew poetry, including translations of Hebrew prayers for the high holy days and translations of religious poems by the medieval poet, Solomon ibn Gabirol.

## I  Blind Children

Zangwill's comments on the relative difficulty of poetry and prose suggest why his poetry lacks artistic merit. In an 1894 column for *The Critic,* he maintains that prose is a more difficult art than poetry: "The swing and rush of verse compensate for reason, and it is wonderful how far a little sense will fly when tricked out with fine feathers."[3] It should be no surprise that an author who believes that the trappings of verse can substitute for precision of thought writes bad poetry. Zangwill was apparently aware of his limitations as poet; for, in the dedicatory poem to his one volume of poems, *Blind Children* (1903), he modestly compares his poems to blind children, "Wistfully haunted by/ That unattainable/ Glamorous sea of light/ True poems float within." Like blind children, his poems go "haltingly,/ Feeling their way to you,/ Tapping their road to Truth,/ Groping their path to God!"[4]

The poems in this volume, Zangwill says, are "the better part of the verses that have accumulated in manuscript or in magazines, journals, and the writer's own books during the last twenty years"; they cover, like Zangwill's essays, almost every subject, and they represent "many moods." For example, the first two poems in the collection illustrate the extremes of disillusion and confident assertion of faith. "Sylva Poetarum" laments, in tetrameter couplets, the loss of poetry and magic in a disenchanted world. The first three sections of the poem evoke the "ancient wood" of enchantment, rest, beauty, and youth, where "The very air is poesy"; the last section describes, in contrast, an "earthly wood," characterized by struggle, pain, and death. This latter world lacks the natural beauty, the supernatural presences, the gods of the ancient enchanted world; in it "Man is left alone with Man."

The bleakness of the modern world is suggested by images of silent stars, stilled music, a dark night, and a chill wind. The contrast between the golden world and the barren world is conveyed by the diction as well as by the images. In Parts I–III, archaic poetic diction is used to describe a "delightsome land," with "white-robed wanderers," "Deep-bosomed Venus," and "tricksy Puck a-frolicking"; in the section describing the loss of poetry, such diction disappears, except in a brief passage referring to "The olden magic" of birds' songs. In short, the structure, images, and diction in "Sylva Poetarum" indicate that Zangwill was technically proficient in suiting theme to form; his poetic failure, as the quotations from the poem ought to illustrate, was in the language. If Zangwill's diction is supposed to suggest the poetry that is forever lost to the world, we are only too glad to say farewell to it.

The second poem in the collection, "At the Worst," is an answer to "Sylva Poetarum." It begins with the last line of "Sylva Poetarum" ("And Man is left alone with Man"), with " 'Tis well!" appended to it. The former age is compared to "childish toys," now outgrown by man, who "wakes to grander fears and hopes and joys"; renewed hope lies in an awakened social consciousness and in a willingness to struggle to understand God. Echoing Romantic philosophy, Zangwill asserts that a higher life and God himself are evolving out of the human struggle with doubts. Significantly, Zangwill's expression of hope relies not on the rebirth of poetry but on a renaissance of human aspiration.

A similar optimism appears in the poem which gives the volume its name. "Blind Children," in free verse, falls into two sections; the first describes joyous but blind children playing on a school lawn, rich in a world of scent, sound, and touch. A question, anticipating the question with which the poem ends, divides the first section, as the poet asks, "How should they know or feel/ They are in darkness?" Then follows a description of a world "New-born in loveliness" which would result from a miraculous redemption of the children. The second section draws an analogy between the children playing and the larger human "dark world," which may also contain "a strange [but hidden] Glory." The poem ends with a question: "Do we sport carelessly,/ Blindly upon the verge/ Of an Apocalypse?" The division in the poem between the dark world, with its blissful ignorance, and the possibility of a glorious world beyond human comprehension once again affirms Zangwill's faith in the existence of both a mundane and a heavenly reality. This dual vision can be seen in many of the poems in *Blind Children,* which includes both poems of disillusionment and ones of hope.

Belonging to the poems of disillusionment are "Sunset," where the setting sun represents the loss of vision and love; "Night Mood," which expresses a mood of horror and hopelessness; and "Dreams," in which the poet dreams "of love and glory" but gets instead "Life's long slow sordid story." "The Sign" succinctly states in four lines the sense of nothingness, the loss of hope, the memory of lost happiness expressed in most of the poems of disillusion:

> The man peers silently into the dim
> Blank eyes of the dead universe with tears,
> Because there is no sign shown unto him
> Save memories of their smile in childish years.

The Italian sonnet "Hinc Illae Lachrymae" also expresses despair and yearning for a lost, "unpossessable" beauty and a youthful, golden dream. At times the poet feels a sense of helplessness and alienation; for example, in "In Mentone" he compares himself to a caged lion; in exile, he is bereft of his mate and his kingdom. Similarly, in "At the Zoo" he empathizes with the caged "tropic creatures," for "I, too, desire the sun and am a slave." Some poems have a bitter, cynical tone: in "Après" the poet burns his poems, disillusioned with women and the world, and then learns "a bitterer truth"—that the world and women are bad *and* "my songs are burnt"; "The Cynic" says that "Fresh hearts" and "the same sweet lies" will return when the cynic is dead, "When God's gag lies on the mouth of me." In these poems the poet finds no hope in prophecy or religion. "The Prophet's Message" is the suicide note of "the Teacher of the Age"; "To the Blessed Christ" says that Christ was blessed in dying before the death of dreams. "A Tabernacle Thought" is equally cheerless: a child in a "Cool Retreat" reaches for lovely fruits and flowers, only to discover gilded fruit and waxen flowers—symbols of life, "a pretty vision" lacking truth.

The poems of disillusionment are offset by those of hope and affirmation. "A Winter Morning's Mood" is a burst of glorious, "magical" vision in the midst of heartsickness; "In the City" is another vision of beauty and goodness "Sudden amid the slush and rain." Like "At the Worst," the poem "Perspective" expresses comfort in the thought of man's strength and creativity, and "The Sense of Justice" finds evidence of God in man's ability to doubt God's existence. In "Why do we Live?" the answer is that "The 'why' cannot be understood/ . . . So let's muse less and do more good." In "Despair and Hope," the hope lies in love.

The power of love is the theme of numerous poems in *Blind Children,* including some of the poems mourning the death of loved ones. In contrast with the grief and despair in poems of death such as "Lost," "In the Morgue," and "Hopeless" are the poems which offer comfort in spite of loss. "Love and Death" contrasts the "weary days" when "memory was misery" (stanza 1) with the days after "a second Birth/ Of Love," when "memory is harmony" (stanza 2); "Death's Transfiguration" contrasts our mean daily lives with the transfiguration that comes when "Death comes in our midst, . . ./ And touches vulgar life with silver light." Other poems reconciling the idea of death with hope are "Forever Young," "With the Dead," and "The Bridge."

The love songs in *Blind Children* consist of celebrations of love and laments for love lost. Among the numerous short love lyrics, "Palingenesis" is one of the most successful. In this blank verse poem, the poet first describes his joyless, faithless, beautyless youth devoted to reason (stanza 1); then he describes his increasing awareness of beauty, of joy, of "life re-born at radiant dawn of Love" (stanza 2). The syntax and the diction of the second stanza

produce the effect of soaring joy: the stanza is one long, uninter-
rupted fragment dominated by words of movement and life and by
light images. In contrast, stanza 1 has syntactic interruptions and
a refrain referring to "no dream/ Of beauty" and "Death's persuasive hand." The same manipulation of contrasting moods
appears in the poems of spring sorrow ("A Spring Thought" and
"Spring in the Strand") and in "Winter," where the indifference
of the loved one makes a promise of springlike joy turn to barren
winter once more.

In addition to the poems of love and death, joy and despair, are
those which celebrate nature. For example, in "A River Rondeau"
a musing, wistful mood is inspired by the gliding moon and starlit
river; in "Pastoral," "A rich-toned landscape" and subdued sunset
bring on a pensive mood; in "Chastity," the poet finds an analogue
between snow falling on a warm and eventually burgeoning earth
and the blossoming "soul/ In sacramental purity arrayed." So, too,
"Sic Transit" finds in twilight rain, morning dew, or the rose scent
of noonday a sense of "diviner dawns and sunsets soul-create."

The poem "A Singer to his Song" suggests the variety of themes
and moods in *Blind Children*. Drawing a comparison between the
child born and the poem created, the poet calls poetry the product
of human sorrow and delight. He alludes (in stanzas 3 and 4)
to the subject of poetry: nature and woman and memories of
childhood glory and lost man; finally, he states again his modest
aspirations—to "Make music for a pleasured age." "Alla Cantatrice" is a better expression of Zangwill's poetic purpose; in this
poem the "songstress" is to "Marry all splendours and wonders
of sunset and morning" (stanza 2), to combine "exquisite moments
of passion and feeling" (stanza 3), to create rapturous song and
dirges (stanza 6), to blend "the chords of pain and delight"
(stanza 8)—in short, to express, as Zangwill aspires to do in all
his work, the tragicomedy of life.

As in his prose, Zangwill produces his most interesting, though
not always his best, poetry on Jewish subjects and themes. Some
of this poetry is almost unbelievably bad: the sonnet on Herzl has
already been alluded to, and the Spenserian sonnet "The Jews
of England (1290–1902)" is another example of good sentiments
in bad verse. The octave of the poem traces the history of Jewish
persecution from Edward II (1290) to Edward VII (1902); the
sestet praises England's martial glory, which can be surpassed by

a nobler victory: the "triumph o'er her own intolerance." A better sonnet on the subject of Christian antipathy toward the Jews is "Moses and Jesus." In this poem the two prophets meet, greet each other with *"Shalom Aleikhem,"* and, as the sounds of a church hymn and synagogue chant blend, look at each other "With bitter tears of agonized despair."

On the subject of Jewish failure is "Israel," with its thematic refrain: "Hear, O Israel, Jehovah, the Lord our God is One,/ But we, Jehovah His people, are dual and so undone." On the same subject but with bitter irony, in which God is blamed as much as his people, is "Israel in Exile: or Harlequin Little Jacob Horner." This sonnet is prefaced by a statement from the *Jewish Chronicle:* "By a coincidence the orthodox Jew will begin the twentieth century with a fast in commemoration of the Siege of Jerusalem." The poem bitterly begins, "A whit long-spun, O Lord," referring to the nineteen hundred years of Jewish suffering which God has permitted. The exile is conceived of as an "epic play,/ 'The Wandering Jew' in nineteen hundred acts"; the poet calls for a "briefer" tragedy and, finally, objects to the elements of pantomime that the long suffering has produced, as the orthodox Jew celebrates (as in a pantomime) his holidays while the tragedy is enacted.

In other poems, religious celebrations are not used as evidence of tragicomic futility but as symbols of romance. In "Asti Spumanti" the wine "works a miracle": it evokes the magic of raisin wine, unleavened bread, and the Passover; and it brings back memories of the "blessedness" of a Jewish childhood. The sonnet "Seder-Night" also finds value in religious ceremony by contrasting the vulgar, noisy world of London streets with the atmosphere of "reverential mirth," quaint customs, and ancient ritual in the Jewish home on the *Seder*. The most ambitious—and successful— of these poems is Zangwill's imitation of Robert Burns's "The Cotter's Saturday Night." Called "The Hebrew's Friday Night. (After Burns)," Zangwill's poem celebrates the transfiguration offered the humble Jew by the Sabbath ritual.

Just as Burns's poem describes the return of the Cotter from his hard week's work to his simple cottage, where love and piety rule, "The Hebrew's Friday Night" describes the return of the Jew from the synagogue to his home prepared for the Sabbath. The poem begins with praises for the "Sweet Sabbath-Bride," which brings forgetfulness of man's mortality and sorrow. Stanzas 3 and 4 depict the father's return to the Sabbath table and his "children's shining faces"; stanzas 5 and 6 describe the ritual of the festive meal, and stanza 7 concludes that the Jew's faith survives "in a thousand squalid Ghettos" because it is rooted in "The simple love of home and child and wife,/ The sweet humanities which make our higher life." Unlike his model, Zangwill omits many of the details of the simple evening at home (the specific Bible stories read and the hymns sung); he compresses Burns's nineteen stanzas into seven; he avoids most of the sentimentalizing of the home scene (the father's homely advice and prayers); and he replaces Burns's idyllic mood with an almost matter-of-fact tone. The effect of Zangwill's alterations is to suggest a commonplace scene which, nevertheless, has its moments of beauty and romance.

## II  *Translations of Hebrew Poetry*

Other religious poems in *Blind Children* include translations from Hebrew poetry—one poem is from the Hebrew of Alchanan ben Isaac, an English Jew of the twelfth century; another is a "Zionist Marching Song. (From the Hebrew of Imber)" (Imber was Zangwill's model for the poet Pinchas in *Children of the Ghetto*); included also are an "Atonement Hymn" by a twelfth-century poet and a translation of a synagogue hymn, "Adon Olam." Zangwill also translated from medieval Jewish poets Hebrew prayers which are still included in the authorized festival prayers of the English Jewish congregation.[5] But Zangwill's best work as translator was his translation of *Selected Religious Poems of Solomon ibn Gabirol,* which was published by the Jewish Publication Society of America in 1923.

In an essay "On Translating Gabirol" Zangwill discusses the nature of the poetry of Gabirol, who was the kind of artist Zangwill admired: a "thinker among poets, and the poet for thinkers."[6] Gabirol wrote poetry of transition, poetry which "was passing from a purely devotional to a secular character." Zangwill finds Gabirol's religious poetry of lasting value; though the view of the cosmos expressed in Gabirol's greatest poem is as scientifically out of date as Dante's, the theology is not, says Zangwill; for "the force that set the planets in motion has never abdicated." Commenting on the problems of translation, Zangwill says that he does

not try to follow Gabirol's "exact verse-schemes"; he is content
if he can get "an analogous effect by the use of English measures
appropriate to his theme." He continues: "To translate him into
bare prose seems to me the only license unpermissible, for poetry
is largely verbal enchantment, and to leave out the singing elements
is to falsify the original even more badly than by mistranslation."[7]

Zangwill's translations of Gabirol are in many respects remarkable renderings into idiomatic English of difficult and sometimes
obscure Hebrew poetry. But too often, in his attempt to retain
"the singing elements," Zangwill turns Gabirol's vigorous eleventh-
century Hebrew poetry into minor nineteenth-century verse. As
an example of Zangwill's technique as translator, we may compare
a literal translation of the first poem in *Selected Religious Poems*
with Zangwill's translation of it. The following is a literal translation of the supplication "At the Dawn":

> At dawn I seek you, my rock and my refuge
>   (fortress, or shelter);
> I prepare a speech for your face (presence), my dawn
>   and also my evening.
> In the face (presence) of your greatness I stand and
>   am astonished (terrified),
> For your eye sees all the thoughts of my heart.
> What is this that the heart and the tongue are able
> To do? And what is the power of my spirit (breath)
>   in the midst of my inner being (literally, entrails)?
> Here to you man's praise (song) may seem good because
> For a time as yet the breath of God is in me.[8]

The following translation is Zangwill's:

> At the dawn I seek Thee,
>   Rock and refuge tried,
> In due service speak Thee
>   Morn and eventide.
> 'Neath Thy greatness shrinking,
>   Stand I sore afraid,
> All my secret thinking
>   Bare before Thee laid.
> Little to Thy glory
>   Heart or tongue can do;
> Small remains the story,
>   Add we spirit too.

> Yet since man's praise ringing
> May seem good to Thee,
> I will praise Thee singing
> While Thy breath's in me.[9]

Gabirol's poem is metrically perfect, with each line conforming to this rhythm: $/ / x / | / / || / / x / | / /$. In the poem the $[i]$ sound predominates in assonance and in the end rhyme $[bi]$. We are not surprised that Gabirol's meter, assonance, and rhyme are lost in Zangwill's translation; and Zangwill admits that he makes no attempt to render the acrostic on Gabirol's name which appears in this and other poems. But we are justifiably disappointed at the general weakening of effect in Zangwill's poem. For example, Zangwill's "refuge tried" for "my refuge" in the original is weak: its reversal of the normal English adjective-noun position strikes us as falsely "poetic"; "tried" is there for the sake of filling out the meter of the line and for the rhyme in line 4. The sense of direct communication with God is lost in the translation of "my dawn and also my evening" to the adverbial "Morn and eventide." And the questions of lines 5–6 in the original are lost in translation.

The opening lines of the second poem in the collection, "My Soul Shall Declare," illustrate a similar loss of immediacy. Zangwill's poem begins, "My soul shall declare to Thee Thou art her former/ And shall Thee as her maker, O God, testify." In Gabirol's poem, the poet speaks simply and directly to God: "To you my soul will talk, for you have made it,/ And it will declare [make known, inform], for with your hand, God, you made it." The rendition of Gabirol's poetry into the diction of formal English also often results in a loss of conciseness, as for example in these lines from "The Messiah" (No. 3):

> Dawn like a flag
> Surmounts the crag
> Of Tabor's hill,
> And its flame it unfurls o'er my
> Hermon, the hoar and chill.

Gabirol's poem says simply: "The dawn/ Has risen like a banner at the top of Tabor and my Hermon." We can justify Zangwill's expansion of the original to explain Tabor and Hermon, but the rest of the details add little to the sense and seem to be there only to fill out lines.

Too often, in fact, Zangwill seems controlled by the formal conventions of his verse; another example is "Invitation" (No. 4), a fairly literal translation in which the sensuous detail is almost lost in the regularity of tetrameter couplets:

> Come up to me at early dawn,
> Come up to me, for I am drawn,
> Beloved, by my spirit's spell,
> To see the sons of Israel.
> For thee, my darling, I will spread
> Within my court a golden bed,
> And I will set a table there
> And bread for thee I will prepare,
> For thee my goblet I will fill
> With juices that my vines distil.[10]

What is finally most striking about Zangwill's translations is that he loses the Old Testament scriptural flavor of the original and creates a conventional hymn.

On the other hand, very often in the Gabirol translations Zangwill is able to turn into idiomatic English Hebrew constructions which simply cannot be translated literally, as in the poem "Ecstasy" (No. 12). In this poem Zangwill translates Gabirol's two-line units into English triplets which capture the joyous, exuberant spirit of the original. And in "Humble of Spirit" (No. 14) he offers a free-verse translation which loses none of the directness and simplicity of Gabirol's statement. This poem shows that Zangwill is at his best as translator when he abandons regular meter and rhyme—those "fine feathers" which he felt could "compensate for reason"—and closely follows the original.

Thus the poem considered Gabirol's best—the *Keter Malkut* ("The Royal Crown," No. 50)—is also Zangwill's best; in it Zangwill abandons rhyme, fixed meter, and regular stanzaic form to concentrate on close translation. Zangwill's own comments on his translation of this long poem explain its success: "In translating the *Keter Malkut,* I have regarded a rhyme-scheme as apt to mislead me from my original. It is noteworthy that in this his greatest poem, Gabirol, though he conserves rhyme largely, throws over the jingle of a fixed metre, as if to give sincerity and spontaneous-ness freer scope."[11] Noting the echo of Gabirol's "Old Testament predecessors" in the poem, Zangwill continues: "trammelled by neither rhyme nor metre, and aiming only at this Old Testament simplicity, I have escaped all temptation to eke out the poet's plain meaning. You might use me as a crib." But, in staying closely with his original, Zangwill creates more than "a crib": he captures the rhythm, the imagery, the biblical echoes of his source, even retaining the quotation from Scripture climaxing the stanzaic structure.

### III  *The Verse of* The War God

In addition to translations of Hebrew poetry and his own poems, Zangwill wrote a blank-verse play, *The War God,* and any examination of Zangwill as poet demands some commentary on the prosody of that play. The critics who saw the 1911 Beerbohm Tree performance complained of the tendency of the verse toward declamation; certainly in the play Zangwill does not always avoid pretentious rhetoric, but he does avoid bombast. For the most part, the verse approximates the rhythms of natural speech and is notable for its absence of aureate diction, rhetorical flourishes, and long speeches. If, occasionally, the characters deliver blank-verse sermons, the fault is more in the nature of the play as an antiwar tract than in the verse form. A brief extract from one of the more declamatory speeches—the chancellor's defense of might in the final act—serves as illustration of Zangwill's verse in the play:

> Dominance—
> There rings the password of the universe.
> Who knows it, he is free of every camp.
> Equality, your level, endless cornfield,
> However fat and fair and golden-stalked,
> Would set us pining for the snow-topped peaks
> And barren glaciers. Life is fight, thank God!
> Come, bare your forehead to the fierce salt Truth.
> Take war away and men would sink to molluscs,
> Limpets that wait the tide to wash them food.
> The nations would grow foul with lazy feeding.
> What Heaven loves is breeds with life a-tingle,
> Swift-gliding, flashing, darting death at rivals,
> Men fearing God and with no other fear.[12]

Syntactically, the passage has variety and a minimum of locutions violating normal grammatical patterns. The diction is precise and simple, except for "molluscs," "Limpets," and the affected "a-tingle." The imagery—for example, the "endless cornfield" of equality and the "peaks" and "glaciers" of dominance—is effective; the device of alliteration, though overused in this passage, is not obtrusive. And, finally, in Zangwill's defense, most of the verse in the play is more subdued than this passage in which the subject (world dominance) and the speaker (a warmonger) could justify bombast. A more representative passage is the Jew Blum's defense of his apostasy:

> Had Christians handled us with Christliness,
> There would not be a single Jew in Europe.
> We should have melted in your love as I
> Have melted in Count Frithiof's.[13]

The verse is prosaic, but the idea is not; indeed, the idea rescues the passage (as it does the play) from failure.

That is not to say that Zangwill is a good poet; this examination of his poetry begins and ends with the admission that he is not. If his reputation as artist had rested on his poetry, he would not have received any recognition at all. In translating Hebrew poetry, Zangwill is at his best when he ceases to write "poetry" and simply translates his source as faithfully as possible. Perhaps that observation alone serves as the last word on Zangwill's failure as poet.

CHAPTER 7

# Dreamers of the Ghetto

Zangwill's present reputation is accurately described by Louis Golding, who says that the name "Zangwill" calls up even to literary people only "a dim recollection of an unfashionable, and therefore unregarded, writer."[1] It is indeed fair to say that to some literary people it does not call up even "a dim recollection." Zangwill's present obscurity can be attributed to the fact that at the turn of the twentieth century he abandoned his exceptional talent for writing short stories and novels and turned instead to writing essays and dramas analyzing and offering solutions to social, political, and religious ills. Thus, his reputation in the twentieth century rested on his journalistic prose and his dramatic offerings, and his strength as an artist was in neither of these.

But to read Zangwill's early fiction today is to discover again the genius that made him famous in the 1890's, a genius for the creation of unforgettable, living characters and for the depiction of scenes and incidents calling up the sordidness, pain, and wonder of everyday reality. In this fiction there is much that deserves to be reintroduced to students of English literature, especially in the ghetto works, *Children of the Ghetto, The King of Schnorrers,* and numerous short stories from *"They that Walk in Darkness"* and *Ghetto Comedies.*

## I Present-day Dreamers

Given the popularity of modern American Jewish writers such as Bernard Malamud, Edward Wallant, Philip Roth, or Saul Bellow, it is ironic that Zangwill has not enjoyed a revival of interest. For we find in the characters, situations, and themes of these writers much that Zangwill treated with equal artistry sixty or seventy years earlier. For example, in Philip Roth's short story "Defender of the Faith," Zangwill's "Luftmensch" appears. A character described by Zangwill as "a Jewish type, assertive that 'all Israel are brethren,' and insistent on its right to travel and study at the fraternal expense,"[2] the "Luftmensch" is the central character in the story of that name and also in *The King of Schnorrers* and "The Model of Sorrows"; in Roth's story the "Luftmensch" is Sheldon Grossbart, a soldier who uses his Jewishness for personal gain in appealing to Sergeant Nathan Marx's own sense of brotherhood in the faith.[3]

The children of the ghetto have moved to Chicago in Saul Bellow's *The Adventures of Augie March* (1953), with its realistic re-creation of Augie's poverty-stricken Jewish childhood. Zangwill's attacks on the hypocrisy and shame of upper-middle-class Jewry are echoed in Philip Roth's "Eli, the Fanatic," where the Jewish suburbanites, like Zangwill's anti-Semitic Jews, are ashamed of Leo Tzuref's school for orphaned refugees in their community and are especially embarrassed by the assistant's black coat, "round-topped, wide-trimmed Talmudic hat, . . . beard . . . [and] sidelocks curled loose on his cheeks."[4] Another modern echo of Zangwill is in Bernard Malamud's *The Assistant* (1958), with its central theme the suffering and self-sacrificing Jew.

The examples of themes and characters common to both Zangwill and modern Jewish novelists could be multiplied; but one more ought to suffice to illustrate my point that Zangwill's work contains much that is popular in literary circles today. I cite Edward Wallant's conclusion to *The Human Season* (1960), a novel which, like Zangwill's best novels, conveys the peculiar richness of a commonplace life; the protagonist, struggling to reconcile himself to the death of his wife, has been speaking throughout the novel to God as to a friend who suddenly betrayed him, causing his faith to collapse. At the end, like Esther Ansell in *Children of the Ghetto,* Wallant's hero can see that

Answers come in little glimmers to your soul, most clearly in childhood, in the sounds of certain voices and faces and things, when you feel the miracle and the wonder; and he knew then that the Torahs and prayer shawls and churches and saints were just the art men tried to create to express the other, deeper feeling.
"It's like a light that don't last long enough to recognize anything. But the light itself, just that you seen it . . . that's got to be enough. . . ." And then more emphatically, almost desperately, for it was his last hope: "It *is* enough!"[5]

This statement is identical to Zangwill's repeated assertion that the greatest value in a Jew's life is the glimpse of beauty and spirituality absorbed in a Jewish childhood.

## II  *Zangwill's Dreamers*

The theme of "the miracle and the wonder" of ordinary life appears in numerous Zangwill works, but never more powerfully than in "Chad Gadya," one of the stories in *Dreamers of the Ghetto* (1898). I have chosen to discuss *Dreamers of the Ghetto,* considered by some to be Zangwill's best work, in this last chapter for three reasons. First, because the collection of stories and portraits illustrates Zangwill's major themes, I can restate those themes by discussing them in a new context. Second, for those readers who read only the conclusion of a book, I would provide an analysis of at least one Zangwill book, one of his best. And, third, the arrangement of chapters by genre left me with no place for *Dreamers of the Ghetto.* It is framed by two short stories, "A Child of the Ghetto" and "Chad Gadya." Most of the other selections are neither short stories nor essays, but fictionalized biographies—or, more accurately, imaginary portraits with a factual basis.

In "Chad Gadya," the last story in the book, the protagonist is a man of the world who has abandoned Judaism; he returns to his Venetian home on *Seder* night, and during the recitation of the song "Chad Gadya," remembers past days of peace and security. Like Wallant's hero, Zangwill's protagonist realizes that "It was atavism that gave him those sudden strange intuitions of God at the scent of a rose, the sound of a child's laughter, the sight of a sleeping city; that sent a warmth to his heart and tears to his eyes, and a sense of the infinite beauty and sacredness of life."[6] Unfortunately, these moments are too rare; he succumbs to despair.

The technique of the story is the progressive unfolding of the protagonist's thoughts and feelings as the ritual song progresses. At first, he simply appreciates the esthetic beauty of the exotic ritual, which becomes merely another artistic experience for him; then a mood of hopelessness overcomes him, as he contrasts his philosophical drifting with the "atmosphere of peace and restfulness and faith and piety" suggested by the *Seder* ritual. Realizing that he is still "a Jew at heart," he is filled with childhood and race memories, which lead him to wonderment at the fact that the Jews have survived while empires have crumbled. This mood is lost, and he finally hears in "Chad Gadya" only evidence of the instability of life and the vanity of existence. In this mood he leaves his father's house and drowns himself, for suddenly "life without God, seemed intolerable." But, at the moment of death, he affirms the unity of God, speaking "the immemorial Hebrew words of the dying Jew."

In the thoughts and feelings of the protagonist we recognize familiar Zangwill themes, especially the theme of the return of the prodigal, treated extensively in *Children of the Ghetto* as well as in Zangwill's short stories about the *Meshummad*. The separation of generations, represented by the pious father and the skeptical, ultimately despairing offspring, is another major Zangwill theme. Zangwill's hostility to organized religion, expressed vehemently in *Italian Fantasies* and in *The Next Religion,* appears in "Chad Gadya" as the protagonist realizes that the Jew has survived by his energy and his will to keep the religious spirit alive, while states and state religions have been defeated (weakened into hollow forms) by their very success. And, finally, Zangwill's belief that art must exert moral force and that philosophy must provide hope is illustrated by the utter failure of the insincere artist and faithless philosopher. The protagonist represents, Zangwill says, "the wandering Jew of the world of soul"—a "modern of moderns, dreamer of dreams, and ponderer of problems" (495). "He stood for latter-day Israel" (501); and he is, Zangwill suggests, lost once he has been cut loose from his father's faith.

Just as the last story in the collection deals with the return of the prodigal, the dreamer who, outside the ghetto, was "like an orphan wind, homeless, wailing about the lost places of the universe" (501), the first story deals with a ghetto child's cutting free, another major Zangwill theme. "A Child of the Ghetto" is set, like "Chad Gadya," in the Venice ghetto, enclosed by walls, water, and gates. The child knows nothing of life outside the ghetto, which is "all his world, and a mighty universe it was; full of everything that the heart of a child could desire" (2). Part I of the story describes Jewish festivals and everyday ceremony, which constitute an "inner world of dreams" for the child. Describing and characterizing the child's ghetto world are words such as "fascination," "delight," "beautiful," "sweet," "restful." Then, in Part II, the child's coming of age is briefly described; and in Part III, he gets his first glimpse of the outside world.

The child leaves the ghetto on the Day of Atonement, the day of the great White Fast; he is awed and disturbed by the active life outside the ghetto, and when he returns to the synagogue, "something of the old passion and fervor had gone out of his voice" (19). The conflict that results from this vision of "a vaster universe without" constitutes the major struggle in *Children* and *Grandchildren of the Ghetto;* for Esther Ansell and other children of the ghetto, Israel Zangwill included, glimpsed through education the life outside and were drawn irresistibly to it. But, at the end of "A Child of the Ghetto," the child is left with "a nameless trouble and vague unrest" in his soul—the same unrest that drives Esther back to the ghetto, that drives the protagonist of "Chad Gadya" to suicide, and that caused Zangwill to identify his values with those of Judaism long after he had broken with orthodoxy. Significantly, in *Children of the Ghetto,* Zangwill has Reb Shemuel, the representative of tradition and changelessness, tell his daughter that "The worst of Jews cannot put off his Judaism. His unborn soul undertook the yoke of the Torah at Sinai."[7]

The notion that a Jew "cannot put off his Judaism" reappears in the fictionalized biographies in *Dreamers of the Ghetto,* and it is expressed most emphatically in the sketch of Heinrich Heine, who says, "I may have worshipped the Madonna in song, for how can a poet be insensible to the beauty of Catholic symbol and ritual? But a Jew I have always been" (354). Heine's dream, in many ways like Zangwill's, was a desire to reconcile Jew and Greek—Hebraism and Hellenism, goodness and beauty—and create a foundation for "the religion of the future"; but God (the "Arch-Humorist") paralyzed the "German Aristophanes," who is condemned to a kind of living death. As he speaks in "From a Mattress Grave," Heine yearns for "the simple faith, the clear vision of the child that holds its father's hand" (347); he dreams of a life in the ghetto, of a home and children sanctified by Judaism. But, in the past, his was a larger dream; like the "Child of the Ghetto," he envisioned "a vaster universe without" and fought in "the Liberation War of Humanity" (343).

The conflict between the ghetto and all it represents and the world outside unifies the biographical portraits in *Dreamers of the Ghetto*. The first two portraits are studies in apostasy. "Joseph the Dreamer" depicts a Roman Jew who converts to Catholicism; "Uriel Acosta," a Portuguese Catholic who converts to Judaism. Both are motivated by a dream of a purer religion: Joseph by the ideal of loving sacrifice at the heart of Christianity; Uriel Acosta by the "sublime and simple" creed of Judaism. Joseph, who discovers that Christians do not practice the Christianity he believes in, is martyred after speaking out against Jew-baiting in Carnival time. Uriel Acosta discovers that he has taken on "a host of minute ordinances far more galling than those of the Church" and, rebelling, is placed under a ban; after recantations and lapses, suffering and persecution, he finally kills himself, "despairing of justice on earth and hopeless of any heaven" (114). Both Joseph and Uriel Acosta are outcasts, acceptable neither to Christians nor to Jews—a terrible commentary on the failure of organized religion to live up to its ideals. Later in *Dreamers of the Ghetto,* Heine comments on the world's failure: *"Ach,* every now and again arises a dreamer who takes the world's lip-faith seriously, and the world tramples on another fool" (361).

The next three biographies in *Dreamers of the Ghetto* are of heretics—specifically, mystics, creators of original religions. "The Turkish Messiah" is about Sabbatai Zevi, who in 1848 declared himself messiah of the Jews. The long story, in the form of three scrolls depicting the history of Zevi, recounts Zevi's rise to fame; his miraculous ability to command disciples; his love for Melisselda, "the Messiah's bride"; and his final conversion to Islam. Told in an objective tone, the emphasis in the story is on Zevi's and his followers' messianic dream. Another kind of dream is represented by the transcendental communion with Being of Spinoza, the central figure in "The Maker of Lenses." Spinoza is portrayed as a loving, peaceful, lonely man, outcast by his people and rejected by the woman he loves because "thou art a Jew." Zangwill says of him, "The first Jew to create an original philosophy, he yet remained a Jew in aiming not at abstract knowledge, but at concrete conduct: and was most of all a Jew in his proclamation of the Unity . . . typical—even by his very isolation—of the race that had cast him out" (205).

Both Zevi's and Spinoza's messages are of joy and freedom; so too is that of the Baal Shem, in "The Master of the Name." In this story, told in first-person narrative by a student and follower of the Baal Shem, Zangwill again contrasts original, sin-

cerely felt religion with organized religion. The message of the
"Master," a "genial old man" who lives a simple, humble life of
prayer and fasting, is that the divine exists in human beauty and
joy; as he says, "Call nothing common or profane; by God's
presence all things are holy" (273). On the other hand, the Master's follower, Rabbi Baer, lives in luxury and, after the Master's
death, "made of the Master's living impulse a code and creed
which grew rigid and dead. And he organized his followers by
external signs—noisy praying, ablutions, white Sabbath robes, and
so forth—so that the spirit died and the symbols remained" (285).
Thus in this sketch, as in all his work, Zangwill expresses hostility
to the empty forms of religion.

The search for an original religion Zangwill finds peculiar to the
Jewish temperament; of "the religion of the future," Heine says:
"Be sure of this, anyhow, that only a Jew will find it. We have the
gift of religion, the wisdom of the ages" (358). All Zangwill's
dreamers are in search of a way of life compatible with their
heritage and their new vision. Some, like Joseph and Uriel Acosta,
try a different religion; others, like Sabbatai Zevi, Spinoza, or the
Baal Shem, create their own mystical religion; others try to keep
the best of both the ghetto and the world outside. This attempt to
retain the best is the theme of "Maimon the Fool and Nathan the
Wise," in which Maimon, a philosopher whose search for knowledge has led him to doubt Judaism, meets Moses Mendelssohn, a
philosopher who has combined "culture and spiritual comfort, to
say nothing of worldly success."

This story restates Zangwill's theme of the collapse of orthodox
Judaism in the modern world. Maimon remains always outside
Judaism, though, like all of Zangwill's doubters, "a synagogue-
tune could always move him to tears" (330). Mendelssohn remains orthodox, developing an "ordered scheme of harmonious
living, . . . adjusting with equal mind the claims of the Ghetto and
the claims of Culture" (332). Maimon on his deathbed realizes
that his search for knowledge has ignored an essential part of
life—the emotion and the will; but he also learns from the priest's
trying to effect a deathbed conversion that Moses' way has also
failed, for Moses' children have become Catholics. They were
caught in "the battle of old and new, grown so fierce that the
pietists denied the reformers Jewish burial; young men scorning
their fathers and crying, 'Culture, Culture; down with the Ghetto';

many in the reaction from the yoke of three thousand years falling into braggart profligacy, many more into fashionable Christianity" (333).

All Zangwill's modern children of the ghetto have this battle as background. The character portraits of Heine, Ferdinand Lassalle, and Benjamin Disraeli in *Dreamers of the Ghetto* are written against that background, as is the sketch, "Dreamers in Congress," depicting the first Zionist Congress. This sketch presents in essence Zangwill's attitudes toward Zionism, including his opposition to the Zionists who insisted on Palestine. Expressing the territorialist ideals which would ultimately lead Zangwill to form the Jewish Territorial Organization, he says: "In any land the Jewish soul could express itself in characteristic institutions, could shake off the long oppression of the ages, and renew its youth in touch with the soil" (435); in the name of the "millions oppressed today," he opposes delay in establishing a Jewish homeland. To illustrate the cruelty of waiting for Palestine, Zangwill wrote the story "A Palestine Pilgrim," which follows "Dreamers in Congress" in the book. In this story Aaron the Pedlar, a Russian Jew in Manchester, hears a Zionist speech and is filled with a dream of Palestine. Consequently, he sells his business and sails for Palestine. After an arduous journey with many hardships, Aaron arrives at Palestine but is refused admittance, for "No Russian Jews may enter Palestine."

This story, an answer to those Zionists willing to wait for Palestine, is the first of four short stories ending *Dreamers of the Ghetto*. The book, typical of much of Zangwill's work, is obviously very loosely structured. Framed by the two ghetto stories, the biographical sketches are unified by the fact that each presents a dreamer—a Jew who is not of this world and hence is usually reviled by it. Chronologically arranged, the sketches culminate in a presentation of the Zionist dream of modern Jewry; then follow three stories, each thematically linked to the larger work because the central figure is a dreamer. "The Palestine Pilgrim" depicts the failure of one dream; "The Conciliator of Christendom," the failure of another, as a boot-maker sacrifices his well-being to an ideal of universal brotherhood. "The Joyous Comrade" also depicts an ideal of brotherhood, as a Jewish artist tells about his vision of Christ as the representative of fellowship and love, "the man of genius protesting against all forms and dogmas that would replace the direct vision and the living ecstasy; not the man of sorrows loving the blankness of underground cells and scourged backs and sexless skeletons, but the lover of warm life, and warm sunlight, and all that is fresh and simple and pure and beautiful" (491).

*Dreamers of the Ghetto* does not end on a joyous note, however; "Chad Gadya" pessimistically suggests the fate of modern Jewry. As Zangwill writes in his Preface, *Dreamers of the Ghetto* "is the story of a Dream that has not come true." But "Chad Gadya" does affirm the necessity of a religious spirit, and its epigraph from Exodus, telling of the Lord's deliverance of his people and promising redemption to the firstborn of Israel, once again illustrates Zangwill's faith in the eventual triumph of the dreamer and his dream.

*Dreamers of the Ghetto* contains, then, most of the ideas to be found in Zangwill's total work. Expressed in it, in addition to the idea of the nobility of the ghetto and its dreamers, are the themes of service and self-sacrifice, of the conflict between the old and the new generations, of the failure of present religions to satisfy modern man's aspirations, of the artist's and the philosopher's power to shape a new world, of the Jews' vision of Zion. There is in addition the feminism of "St. Giulia and Female Suffrage" and of *Jinny the Carrier* in the Baal Shem's message in "The Master of the Name": "We err grievously in disesteeming our women: they should be our comrades and not our slaves" (281). There is in "Maimon the Fool" even the tragi-comic schnorrer, who persuades Maimon to beg with him, exclaiming when he sees the poor philosopher, "What a waste of good rags!" (301). Above all, there is the sense of mission—the desire to convert men to a religion of reason and brotherly love—inspiring *Dreamers of the Ghetto* and the whole of Zangwill's work.

*Dreamers of the Ghetto* fails to provide instances of Zangwill's greatest artistry, but to compensate for this, it lacks Zangwill's major literary offenses—garrulity and failures in diction. Zangwill created greater characters in his short stories and novels, and his plays have better structure. There is more comic brilliance in *The King of Schnorrers* and more biting satire in *The Premier and the Painter* and more potent social criticism in the political plays. On the other hand, *Dreamers of the Ghetto* contains some of Zangwill's best short stories and the most sustained expression of his own religious vision. Reviews of the book in 1898 were, for the most part, enthusiastic. "From now on," one reviewer wrote, "Mr. Zangwill must be taken seriously."[8] What the reviewer could not have known was that the promising writer was at the apogee of his literary fame. His next novel, *The Mantle of Elijah,* was also his worst; and his plays and essays of the twentieth century, though interesting, never rose to the level of the ghetto fiction of the 1890's. However, that fiction alone ought to assure a place in English literature for a man generally recognized as "the greatest English Jew of his time."[9]

# Notes and References

## Chapter One

1. G. B. Burgin, "Israel Zangwill: Dramatist and Novelist," *Harper's Weekly*, XXXVIII (June 2, 1894), 508.

2. Laurence Hutton, "Literature Notes," *Harper's Magazine*, XCI (Aug. Supplement, 1895), 4.

3. Quoted in Burgin, p. 508.

4. E. Elzass, quoted in "The Dickens of the Ghetto," *The Review of Reviews*, XII (Nov., 1895), 604; "Mr. Zangwill's Discussions," *Spectator*, LXXVIII (Jan. 2, 1897), 21; "Fiction" (anon. rev. of *The Mantle of Elijah*), *Academy*, LIX (Nov. 17, 1900), 466; Lucien Wolf, "Literature Portraits—XXXII. Mr. Israel Zangwill," *Literature*, IX (Dec. 14, 1901), 549-50; Ernest Radford, "Blind Children," *Bookman* (London), XXIV (Sept., 1903), 216; G. B. Burgin, "Israel Zangwill As I know Him," *Critic*, XLII (Mar., 1903), 268.

5. In The Victorian Era Series (London, 1899), p. 229.

6. Garland, "Israel Zangwill," *Conservative Review* (Washington), II (Nov., 1899), 405.

7. "Roadside Meetings of a Literary Nomad," *Bookman* (New York), LXXI (June, 1930), 304-7.

8. See, e.g., M. J. Landa, "Israel Zangwill, The Dreamer Awake," *Contemporary Review*, CXXX (Aug., 1926), 316-32, who calls Zangwill "the one undoubted literary genius produced by Anglo-Jewry."

9. Simon Pure, "The Londoner," *Bookman* (New York), LXIV (Oct., 1926), 180.

10. In *The Nineteenth Century and After,* by Samuel C. Chew and Richard D. Altick, rev. ed. (New York, 1967), p. 1493.

11. Meyer Waxman, *A History of Jewish Literature,* IV (New York, 1960), 617-18.

12. "Notes," *Nation*, LXXX (June 1, 1905), 441.

13. Bernard N. Schilling, "On Jewish Humor," Pref. *The King of Schnorrers* (Hamden, Conn., 1953), pp. vii-ix.

14. Proem, *Children of the Ghetto* (New York, 1899), p. ix.

15. *The Eighteen Nineties: A Review of Art and Ideas at the Close of the Nineteenth Century* (New York, 1966), p. 27. See Helmut E.

Gerber, "The Nineties: Beginning, End, or Transition?" in *Edwardians and Late Victorians,* English Institute Essays (New York, 1960), pp. 50-70, for the best essay on the complex character of the 1890's.

16. Maurice Wohlgelernter, *Israel Zangwill: A Study* (New York, 1964), pp. 38-40.

17. Dr. Chaim Weizmann's Statement to the Palestine Royal Commission in 1936, quoted in Joseph Leftwich, *Israel Zangwill* (New York, 1957), p. 197. For a discussion of Zangwill's Zionist activities, see Leftwich, pp. 181-215.

18. Quoted in Leftwich, p. 215.

19. Wohlgelernter, p. 12.

20. Jackson, p. 40.

21. John Gross, "Zangwill in Retrospect," *Commentary,* XXXVIII (Dec., 1964), 54.

### Chapter Two

1. *Ibid.,* p. 55.

2. "Literature Portraits—XXXII. Mr. Israel Zangwill," p. 549.

3. "My First Book," *The Idler,* IV (July, 1893), 638.

4. *Ibid.* In addition to the regular columns Zangwill wrote, Zangwiil published essays in *The Independent* (New York), *The New Republic, Outlook* (London and New York), *The Menorah Journal, Fortnightly Review, Jewish Quarterly Review, Bookman* (New York), *Nation* (London and New York), *The English Review,* and others.

5. "Men, Women and Books," *Critic,* XXII, n.s. (Sept. 15, 1894), 166.

6. "Men, Women and Books," *Critic,* XXII, n.s. (Oct. 20, 1894), 251.

7. "The Realistic Novel," *Without Prejudice* (New York, 1897), p. 85. Future references to this book are to this edition.

8. "Men, Women and Books," *Critic,* XXII, n.s. (Nov. 24, 1894), 343.

9. "Men, Women and Books," *Critic,* XXIII, n.s. (June 22, 1895), 452.

10. "Men, Women and Books," *Critic,* XXII, n.s. (Sept. 15, 1894), 165. See also "Pater and Prose," *Without Prejudice,* pp. 207-19.

11. *"Without Prejudice," Bookman* (New York), IV (Feb., 1897), 554-55.

12. "Note," *Nation* (New York), XCI (Dec. 29, 1910), 638.

13. *Italian Fantasies* (New York, 1910), p. 88. Future references to this book are to this edition.

14. There is justice in the *Spectator* reviewer's observation that in *Italian Fantasies* Zangwill is not writing of Italy but of almost every

other conceivable subject ("Mr. Zangwill's Fantasies," *Spectator,* CVI [May 20, 1911], 772).

15. *The War for the World* (New York, 1921), p. 129. Future references to this book are to this edition.

16. *The Principle of Nationalities* (New York, 1917), pp. 84-85, 99, 110.

17. See esp. "The Military Pacifists," pp. 213-20.

18. P. 121. See also "Patriotism and Percentage," pp. 255-64, a parable satirizing the role of modern commerce in war.

19. See esp. "The War Devil," pp. 79-87.

20. Reprinted in *The Voice of Jerusalem* (New York, 1921), pp. 137-51. All my references to *The Voice of Jerusalem* are to this edition.

21. P. 16. Two years earlier, in his speech *Chosen Peoples,* Zangwill had said that characteristic of a chosen people is not "self-sufficient superiority" but "apostolic altruism."

### Chapter Three

1. *The Idler,* IV (July, 1893), 629-41.

2. *Ibid.,* p. 636. Zangwill says that he wrote seven-eighths of the book.

3. *The Premier and the Painter: A Fantastic Romance.* (Chicago, 1896), p. 186. Future references to this work are to this edition.

4. William Morton Payne, "Recent Fiction," *Dial,* XXI (July 1, 1896), 18.

5. *Ibid.*

6. The words are in description of a young satirist, Oudeis, who is also described as "a man to whom Truth was indeed a friend, but Epigram a boon companion . . . a *causeur"* who "had apparently not succeeded in inspiring himself to sufficient flights of dulness to satisfy an English audience" (*The Premier and the Painter,* p. 47).

7. "My First Book," p. 639.

8. *The Bachelors' Club* (New York, 1891), p. 12. Future references to this work are to this edition unless otherwise indicated.

9. *The Celibates' Club: Being the United Stories of The Bachelors' Club and The Old Maids' Club* (New York, 1905), pp. 339-40. Future references to *The Old Maids' Club* are to this edition.

10. *The Old Maids' Club,* pp. 423, 455.

11. Wolf, "Literature Portraits—XXXII. Mr. Israel Zangwill," p. 549.

12. *Children of the Ghetto: A Study of a Peculiar People* (New York, 1899), p. 17. Future references to this work are to this edition.

13. Dan Jacobson, "Jewish Writing in English," Cor:mentary, XXXVII (May, 1964), 49.

14. *The King of Schnorrers* (Hamden, Conn.: Shoe String Press, 1953), p. vii.

15. *The King of Schnorrers* (New York: Dover, 1965), p. xiv.

16. Schilling, pp. xvi-xviii.

17. *The King of Schnorrers: Grotesques and Fantasies* (New York, 1925), p. 50. Future references to this novel are to this edition.

18. Introduction to the Dover edition, p. xiv.

19. Wohlgelernter's account of this final incident contains a factual error. According to Wohlgelernter, Manasseh promises "to contribute to the synagogue the unbelievable sum of six hundred pounds, which he later extorts from a whole series of victims" (Introduction, *The King of Schnorrers,* Dover edition, p. xii). But in fact Manasseh promises one hundred pounds, more than anyone has ever pledged, collects sixty pounds by schnorring, then has Grobstock invest it, where it becomes six hundred. Manasseh then pays his pledge and gives the remaining five hundred pounds to the Da Costa Fund. This latter detail is another indication of Manasseh's character: he could have simply kept the five hundred pounds, but he instead set up the fund, apparently only to gain another triumph of wit over the Elders.

20. Introduction to the Dover edition, p. xiv.

21. *The Master* (New York, 1895), p. 83. Future references to this work are to this edition.

22. *The Master,* p. 316. It is hard to tell whether it is Matt Stang or Zangwill who misinterprets Arnold's poem, which contrasts the vigorous, colorful, romantic world of the merman with the dreary, monotonous, pious life of the woman who forsook him.

23. *The Mantle of Elijah* (New York, 1901), p. 151. Future references to this work are to this edition.

24. Margaret's Christianity cannot be taken as the novel's values, however, for she is also aristocratic, traditionalist, and convinced that war can be a civilizing factor.

25. *Jinny the Carrier: A Folk-Comedy of Rural England* (New York, 1919), p. v. Future references to this work are to this edition.

26. George Saintsbury, "New Novels," *Academy,* XLVII (June 29, 1895), p. 541.

## Chapter Four

1. "'They that Walk in Darkness,'" *Bookman* (London), XVII (Jan., 1900), 118.

2. Meyer Waxman, *A History of Jewish Literature,* IV, 619.

3. *Ghetto Tragedies* (London, 1893), p. 225.

4. *"They that Walk in Darkness": Ghetto Tragedies* (New York, 1899), p. 8.

5. *Ibid.,* p. 66.

6. *Ibid.,* p. 74.

7. *Ibid.,* p. 342.

8. *Ghetto Comedies* (New York, 1929), p. 55.

9. *Ibid.,* p. 274.

10. *Ibid.,* p. 300. All my references to this story are to this edition.

11. *The King of Schnorrers: Grotesques and Fantasies* (New York, 1925), pp. 179, 181.

12. *Ghetto Tragedies,* p. 154.

13. *Ghetto Comedies,* p. 394. Though they do not appear in the story, the words recited in the *Seder* ceremony as the door is opened for Elijah are relevant to the theme of this story: "Pour out Thy wrath upon the heathen that know Thee not and upon the kingdoms that call not on Thy name; for they have devoured Jacob and laid waste his habitation (Psalm 79:6). Pour out upon them Thy fury, and let the heat of Thine anger overtake them (Psalm 69:24). Pursue them in anger, and destroy them from under the heavens of the LORD (Lamentations 3:66)." The goblet is not only a symbol of welcome to Elijah but "a symbol of the 'cup of ruling' which he will give the heathen to drink, and also of the 'cup of comfort' which will be quaffed by Israel." See Theodor Herzel Gaster, *Passover: Its History and Traditions* (Boston, 1962), p. 65.

14. *Ghetto Comedies,* pp. 402-3. All my references to this story are to this edition.

15. *Ibid.,* p. 122. All my references to this story are to this edition.

16. *"They that Walk in Darkness,"* pp. 121-22.

17. *Ibid.,* pp. 120-21.

18. *Ghetto Comedies,* pp. 486-87.

19. *The King of Schnorrers: Grotesques and Fantasies,* p. 204.

20. *Ibid.,* p. 175.

21. *The Grey Wig: Stories and Novelettes* (New York, 1905), p. 34.

22. *Ibid.,* p. 43. Wohlgelernter's résumé of this story in *Israel Zangwill: A Study* (New York, 1964), pp. 90-91, is erroneous; consequently, his conclusion that "these figures are deluded by visions of beauty and grandeur, seeking amid their ruins . . . love" is also erroneous. The old women have no "visions of beauty and grandeur"; they are ashamed because they are too poor to grow old gracefully, with dignity. Ironically, when they acquire the symbol of that ·dignity, the gray wig, their friendship is wrecked; and friendship and love, the story concludes, is more important than grace or dignity.

23. *Ibid.,* p. 127.

24. *Ibid.,* p. 563.

25. This story is discussed in detail in "Zangwill's Plays Pleasant and Unpleasant," below in Ch. 5, Section I.

26. "Recent Novels" (anon. rev. of *"They that Walk in Darkness"*), *Nation,* LXX (Mar. 29, 1900), 245.

27. *Ghetto Comedies,* pp. 327-28.

## Chapter Five

1. Gross, "Zangwill in Retrospect," p. 55.

2. For a history of Zangwill's career as dramatist, see Leftwich, *Israel Zangwill,* pp. 240-73. In this chapter I confine my comments to those plays which should be available in most large university libraries.

3. Wohlgelernter, *Israel Zangwill: A Study,* p. 37.

4. T. M. Parrott, "Israel Zangwill—Playwright," *Booklover's Magazine,* IV (Aug., 1904), 233.

5. It was filmed by Fox Film Corp. in 1916 (five reels, written and pictured by John G. Adolfi and John W. Kellette), in 1920 (five reels, scenario and direction by Edward J. LeSaint), and in 1931 (screenplay by Jules Furthman).

6. *Merely Mary Ann: Comedy in Four Acts* (New York, 1921), p. 19. All my references to this play are to this edition. The short story is in *The Grey Wig* (New York, 1903), pp. 314-445.

7. Quoted from *The Evening Post,* in "Zangwill's Vision of the Great American Melting-Pot," *Literary Digest,* XXXIX (Sept. 18, 1909), 440. For a brief résumé of early critical opinion of the play, see also "Mr. Zangwill's New Dramatic Gospel," *Current Literature,* XLV (Dec., 1908), 671-73, and "Chronicle and Comment," *Bookman* (New York), XXX (Dec., 1909), 324-27.

8. Quoted in Zangwill's Afterword (Jan., 1914) to *The Melting Pot: Drama in Four Acts* (New York, 1917), p. 199.

9. *The Melting Pot,* pp. 33-34. All my references to this play are to the edition of 1917.

10. J. E. Harold Terry, "'The Melting Pot,'" *British Review,* VI (May, 1914), 310.

11. The anonymous reviewer of "Plays of the Month" (*Theatre Magazine,* X [Oct., 1909], 107) found this joke in bad taste. Zangwill uses it to show Kathleen's innocent desire to amuse Frau Quixano; Quincy Davenport and Vera are shocked by Kathleen's line, but that is no reason we should be. It is a good example of the self-directed jokes associated with Jewish humor.

12. *The War God: A Tragedy in Five Acts* (New York, 1912), p. 78. All my references to this play are to this edition.

13. Wohlgelernter, *Israel Zangwill: A Study,* pp. 275-81.

14. *The Next Religion: A Play in Three Acts* (New York, 1913), p. 14. All my references to this play are to this edition.

15. Bernard Shaw, Pref. *Major Barbara* (London, 1931), p. 241.

16. *The Next Religion* was also obviously influenced by Mrs. Humphrey Ward's *Robert Elsmere.* Elsmere, like Trame, founds a new religion after he gives up the Anglican church.

17. *Major Barbara,* p. 328. In the screen version of the play (Baltimore, 1951, p. 133), Shaw makes the "William Morris Labor Temple" in Undershaft's village like the vestry of Saint Thomas' Temple, with busts of the saints of a new religion: Morris ("Saint William of Kelmscott"), "Robert Owen, Marx and Engels and Ferdinand Lassalle, Wells and Shaw and the Webbs; Hyndman and Cunninghame Graham and Kropotkin; Tolstoy and some new Russians called Bolsheviks: all of them the reddest of Reds."

18. *Plaster Saints: A High Comedy in Three Movements* (New York, 1915), p. 197. All my references to this play are to this edition.

19. Matt. 23:27-28; King James Version.

20. In *Too Much Money: A Farcical Comedy in Three Acts* (New York, 1924), p. v. All my references to this play are to this edition.

21. *The Cockpit: Romantic Drama in Three Acts* (New York, 1921), p. 32. All my references to this play are to this edition.

22. *The Forcing House, or The Cockpit Continued: Tragi-Comedy in Four Acts* (New York, 1923), p. 92. All my references to this play are to this edition.

23. "We Moderns," *Theatre Magazine,* XXXIX (May, 1924), 19.

24. *We Moderns: A Post-War Comedy in Three Movements* (New York, 1926), pp. 23-26. All my references to this play are to this edition.

## Chapter Six

1. For example, in *Lippincott's Magazine, Bookman* (New York and London), *The Century Magazine, Critic, Current Literature, Lamp, The Menorah Journal, Journal of Education, Popular Educator* (Boston), and others.

2. Harold Fisch, "Israel Zangwill," *Judaism,* XV (Winter, 1966), 127.

3. "Men, Women and Books," *Critic,* XXII, n.s. (Sept. 15, 1894), 165. Zangwill believes that the prose writer, "like an actor without properties," must rely on his individual perception of rhythm and ornament, and hence must work harder than a poet in creating art. To Zangwill prose was "the highest of all literary forms, the most

difficult of all to handle triumphantly" (*Without Prejudice* [New York, 1897], p. 215).

4. "Ad Unum," in *Blind Children* (London, 1903). All my quotations from Zangwill's poems are from this edition unless I specify otherwise.

5. See, e.g., *Service of the Synagogue: New Year. A New Edition of the Festival Prayers with an English Translation in Prose and Verse* (New York, n.d.). Several of Zangwill's translations in the festival prayers appear in *The Voice of Jerusalem,* pp. 152-65, under "Songs of the Synagogue." Zangwill says that these poems "are designed to elucidate Judaism by illustrating the conceptions that found their way into the orthodox liturgy" (*The Voice of Jerusalem,* p. 152).

6. Quoted by Zangwill from Heine, in "On Translating Gabirol," *Selected Religious Poems of Solomon ibn Gabirol,* ed. Israel Davidson (Philadelphia, 1944), pp. xlv-xlvi.

7. "On Translating Gabirol," pp. xlvi-xlvii, lix, 1.

8. Words in parentheses indicate other possible meanings.

9. This and all my quotations of Zangwill's translations are from the 1944 reprint of *Selected Religious Poems of Solomon ibn Gabirol.*

10. Compare the following translation of the original:

> At dawn come up to me, my beloved; and go with me,
> For my spirit thirsts to see the sons of my people.
> Let me spread for you beds of gold in my entrance hall;
> I will set for you a table; I will arrange for you my feast;
> A cup I will fill for you from grapes of my vineyard.

11. This and the quotation after it are from "On Translating Gabirol," pp. li-lii.

12. *The War God* (New York, 1912), p. 131.

13. *Ibid.,* p. 145.

## Chapter Seven

1. "The Poet of the Ghetto," *Reconstructionist,* XXIV (Apr. 4, 1958), 28.

2. *The Voice of Jerusalem* (New York, 1921), p. 2.

3. In *Goodbye, Columbus, and Five Short Stories* (New York, 1963), pp. 116-43.

4. In *Goodbye, Columbus,* p. 183. It is the same rejection of Jewishness that Benjamin Ansell expresses in *Children of the Ghetto* (New York, 1899), p. 171; Benjy is speaking of his father: "but he might look decent. Does he still wear those two beastly little curls at the side of his head? Oh, I did hate it when I was at school here,

and he used to come to see the master about something. Some of the boys had such respectable fathers."

5. Berkeley Medallion Book (New York, 1964), pp. 159-60.

6. *Dreamers of the Ghetto* (Philadelphia, 1943), p. 503. All my references to this work are to this edition.

7. *Children of the Ghetto,* p. 231.

8. William Morton Payne, "Recent Fiction," *Dial,* XXV (Aug. 1, 1898), 79.

9. Golding, p. 29.

# Selected Bibliography

Most of Israel Zangwill's work was published by William Heinemann in London and by The Macmillan Company in the United States. Until 1969, when AMS Press, Inc., reprinted *The Collected Works,* almost all his work was out of print, and it is still not readily available to the general public. Most of us have to read Zangwill in whatever edition we can find at the nearest large library. The following bibliography lists the editions which I used in my study; if, as is often the case, the edition I used is not the first, I include (in parentheses) publishing information about the first edition. I make no attempt to list any but the most important of the hundreds of periodical articles Zangwill wrote. A more complete listing of Zangwill's works is in Peterson's "Israel Zangwill: A Selected Bibliography" (see below).
1. Essays and Speeches by Israel Zangwill
*Chosen Peoples: The Hebraic Ideal "Versus" the Teutonic.* London: G. Allen & Unwin, Ltd., 1918.
"English Judaism: A Criticism and a Classification," *Jewish Quarterly Review* (London), I (1889), 376-407.
"Fiction as the Highest Form of Truth" (lecture given in the United States in 1899), excerpted in *Bookman* (New York), IX (Apr., 1899), 100-101.
"Ibn Gabirol: Poetry and Philosophy," in *The Menorah Treasury, Harvest of Half a Century.* Edited by Leo W. Schwartz. Philadelphia: The Jewish Publication Society of America, 1964. Pp. 111-20.
*Italian Fantasies.* New York: The Macmillan Company, 1910. (London: William Heinemann, 1910.)
"The Jew in Drama," *Bookman* (New York), XXXIX (June, 1914), 412-13.
"Men, Women and Books," *Critic* (New York) (column appearing monthly, 1894–96).
"Morour and Charousoth," *Jewish Standard* (London) (column appearing irregularly under pseud. "Marshallik," 1888–91).
"My First Book," *The Idler,* IV (July, 1893), 629-41.

## Selected Bibliography

*The Principle of Nationalities* (Conway Memorial Lecture). New York: The Macmillan Company, 1917.

*The Voice of Jerusalem.* New York: The Macmillan Company, 1921. (London: William Heinemann, 1920.)

*The War for the World.* New York: The American Jewish Book Company, 1921. (London: William Heinemann, 1916.)

*Watchman, What of the Night?* New York: American Jewish Congress, 1923.

"When I Am Dead," *Outlook* (New York), CXLIII (Aug. 11, 1926), 502-3.

"Without Prejudice," *Pall Mall Magazine* (London) (monthly column, 1893–96).

*Without Prejudice.* New York: The Century Co., 1897. (London: T. Fisher Unwin, 1896.)

## 2. Novels and Short Stories

*The Bachelors' Club.* New York: Brentano's, 1891. (London: Henry & Co., 1891.)

*The Celibates' Club: Being the United Stories of The Bachelors' Club and The Old Maids' Club.* New York: The Macmillan Company, 1905. (London: William Heinemann, 1898.)

*Children of the Ghetto: A Study of a Peculiar People.* New York: The Macmillan Company, 1899. (Philadelphia: The Jewish Publication Society of America, 1892.)

*Dreamers of the Ghetto.* Philadelphia: Jewish Publication Society of America, 1943. (London: William Heinemann, 1898.)

*Ghetto Comedies.* New York: The Macmillan Company, 1929. (London: William Heinemann, 1907.)

*Ghetto Tragedies.* London: McClure & Co., 1893.

*The Grey Wig: Stories and Novelettes.* New York: The Macmillan Company, 1903. (London: William Heinemann, 1903.)

*Jinny the Carrier: A Folk-Comedy of Rural England.* New York: The Macmillan Company, 1919.

*The King of Schnorrers.* New York: Dover Publications, Inc., 1965.

*The King of Schnorrers: Grotesques and Fantasies.* New York: The Macmillan Company, 1925. (London: William Heinemann, 1894.)

*The Mantle of Elijah: A Novel.* New York: Harper & Brothers Publishers, 1901. (London: William Heinemann, 1900.)

*The Master: A Novel.* New York: Harper & Brothers Publishers, 1895. (London: William Heinemann, 1895.)

*The Premier and the Painter: A Fantastic Romance.* In collaboration with Louis Cowen. Chicago: Rand, McNally & Company, 1896. (London: Spencer Blackett, 1888.)

"A Rose of the Ghetto," in *The English Short Story in Transition.* Edited by Helmut E. Gerber. New York: Pegasus, 1967. Pp. 204-16. (Originally in *The King of Schnorrers: Grotesques and Fantasies.*)

*"They That Walk in Darkness": Ghetto Tragedies.* New York: The Macmillan Company, 1899. (London: William Heinemann, 1899.)

## 3. Plays

*The Cockpit: Romantic Drama in Three Acts.* New York: The Macmillan Company, 1921. (London: William Heinemann, 1921.)

*The Forcing House or The Cockpit Continued: Tragi-Comedy in Four Acts.* New York: The Macmillan Company, 1923. (London: William Heinemann, 1922.)

*The Melting Pot: Drama in Four Acts.* New York: The Macmillan Company, 1917. (New York: The Macmillan Company, 1909.)

*Merely Mary Ann: Comedy in Four Acts.* New York: Samuel French Publisher, 1921. (New York: The Macmillan Company, 1904.)

*The Next Religion: A Play in Three Acts.* New York: The Macmillan Company, 1913. (London: William Heinemann, 1912.)

*Plaster Saints: A High Comedy in Three Movements.* New York: The Macmillan Company, 1915. (London: William Heinemann, 1914.)

*Too Much Money: A Farcical Comedy in Three Acts.* New York: Samuel French, Publisher, 1925. (London: William Heinemann, 1924.)

*The War God: A Tragedy in Five Acts.* New York: The Macmillan Company, 1912. (London: William Heinemann, 1911.)

*We Moderns: A Post-War Comedy in Three Movements (Allegro, Andante, Adagio).* New York: The Macmillan Company, 1926. (London: William Heinemann, 1925.)

## 4. Poems

*Blind Children.* London: William Heinemann, 1903.

*Selected Religious Poems of Solomon ibn Gabirol.* Translated by Israel Zangwill. Edited by Israel Davidson. Philadelphia: Jewish Publication Society of America, 1944. (Originally published 1923.)

## 5. Collections

*Speeches, Articles and Letters of Israel Zangwill.* Edited by Maurice Simon. London: The Soncino Press, 1937.

*The Collected Works of Israel Zangwill.* 14 vols. New York: AMS Press, Inc., 1969.

*The Works of Israel Zangwill.* 14 vols. Edited by A. A. Wolmark. New York: American Jewish Book Co., 1921. (Deluxe edition London: Globe Publishing Co., 1926; New York: The Jewish Book Co., 1931.)

SECONDARY SOURCES

In selecting items from the hundreds of reviews, biographical sketches, interviews, and sections of books devoted to Zangwill, I have given priority to items pertaining to Zangwill's artistic achievement, excluding reviews of single works and books with only passing references to Zangwill. For a more complete bibliography, I refer the reader to my selected annotated bibliography of works about Zangwill, in *English Literature in Transition* (XIII, 1970, 209-44).

1. Books

ADCOCK, A. ST. JOHN. *Gods of Modern Grub Street: Impressions of Contemporary Authors.* London: Sampson Low, Marston & Co., Ltd., 1923; pp. 313-20. Praises Zangwill highly as artist and social critic, placing most value on the ghetto fiction.

BAKER, ERNEST A. *The History of the English Novel.* Vol. IX. London: H. F. & G. Witherby Ltd., 1938; pp. 235-36. Briefly discusses in chapter on "Aesthetes and Eclectics" Zangwill as slum novelist, Jewish novelist, and local color artist.

LEFTWICH, JOSEPH. *Israel Zangwill.* New York: Thomas Yoseloff, 1957. Only recent book-length biography of Zangwill. Without an index and somewhat disorganized, it is hard to use as a reference, but it provides valuable information about Zangwill's life and work.

LOWREY, DWIGHT M. *Mr. Zangwill and the Jew.* Philadelphia: University of Pennsylvania Phi Beta Kappa Society, 1900. An appreciation of Zangwill's impartial depiction of Jewish character and life. Compares Zangwill's Realism favorably with Dickens'; analyzes Zangwill's humor as peculiarly Jewish.

MODDER, MONTAGU FRANK. *The Jew in the Literature of England to the End of the Nineteenth Century.* Philadelphia: The Jewish Publication Society of America, 1939; pp. 333-43, *et passim.* (Also New York: Meridian Books, Inc., 1960.) Analyzes Zangwill's ghetto fiction, stressing the conflict between the old and new life and the absence of stereotyped Jews in his work. Also provides a helpful discussion of Jewish character types and those who oppose them in nineteenth-century English fiction.

OLIPHANT, JAMES. *Victorian Novelists.* The Victorian Era Series. London: Blackie & Son, Limited, 1899; pp. 241-48. Devotes a chapter

to "Rudyard Kipling and I. Zangwill" because each is a Realist dealing with a new subject area and each "gives promise of high
achievement."

SCHILLING, BERNARD N. *The Comic Spirit: Boccaccio to Thomas
Mann*. Detroit: Wayne State University Press, 1965. Two chapters
on *The King of Schnorrers*. Essentially reprints Schilling's essay
"On Jewish Humor" (see below).
————. Preface "On Jewish Humor." In *The King of Schnorrers*.
Hamden, Conn.: The Shoe String Press, 1953; pp. vii-xxxiii. Char-
acterizes Jewish humor: born out of suffering, commenting on the
ludicrous in life, miraculously affirming life in the midst of frus-
tration. Excellent analysis of Manasseh's character (*The King of
Schnorrers*).
SINGER, ISIDORE, ed. *The Jewish Encyclopedia*. Vol. XII. New York:
Ktav Publishing House, Inc., 1964; pp. 633-35. (Also New York:
Funk and Wagnalls Company, 1906.) Most detailed encyclopedia
entry about Zangwill. Includes brief criticism of his work and a
short bibliography.
SPIRE, ANDRÉ. *Israël Zangwill*. Ser. 11, No. 5. Paris: Cahiers de la
Quinzaine, 1909. Sympathetic critical evaluation of Zangwill's
ghetto works, with chapters on Jewish humor and the Jewish Terri-
torial Organization as well. (In French)
————. *Quelques juifs: Israel Zangwill—Otto Weininger—James Dar-
mesteter*. Paris: Société du Mercure de France, 1913; pp. 17-155.
Reprints Spire's earlier work on Zangwill (see above), expanding
the chapter on Zangwill's Zionist activities and adding a chapter on
*Italian Fantasies*.
WAXMAN, MEYER. *A History of Jewish Literature*. Vol. IV. New York:
Thomas Yoseloff, 1960; pp. 617-27. Informative description of life
in English ghettos of the 1880's and 1890's. Discusses Zangwill's
ghetto works against this background.
WOHLGELERNTER, MAURICE. *Israel Zangwill: A Study*. New York: Columbia University Press, 1964. "A sort of biography of Zangwill's
mind." Contains some critical analysis of Zangwill's work but concentrates on his ideology, with sections on his background, his place
in the late nineteenth-century milieu, his place in the Zionist movement, his art theory and political philosophy, and his religious views.
Selected bibliography.

## 2. Periodical Articles

BENSUSAN, S. L. "Israel Zangwill," *Quarterly Review*, CCXLVII (Oct.,
1926), 285-303. Contains a résumé of Zangwill's works, with
appreciative critical comments, and a character sketch emphasizing
Zangwill's selflessness.

BURGIN, G. B. "Israel Zangwill as I Know Him," *Critic*, XLII (Mar., 1903), 266-69. Reminisces about the days when "we were all marching . . . under the banner of 'The New Humour' "; provides firsthand information about Zangwill's wit, appearance, and character.

EISENSTEIN, IRA. "Israel Zangwill," *Reconstructionist*, XVII (June 1, 1951), 17-21. (Also in *Jewish Book Annual*, X [1951–52], 37-42.) Pleads for a reinstatement of Zangwill to prominence among modern Jews, who now have "nicely-bound [but unread] sets of the 'Works.' " Good analysis of Zangwill's major themes.

FISCH, HAROLD. "Israel Zangwill," *Judaism*, XV (Winter, 1966), 126-28. Review of Wohlgelernter's *Israel Zangwill: A Study* and the Dover edition of *The King of Schnorrers*. Evaluates Zangwill as artist; calls for a revival of the ghetto novels.

GARLAND, HAMLIN. "I. Zangwill," *Conservative Review* (Washington, D.C.), II (Nov., 1899), 404-12. Traces the enthusiastic reception of Zangwill in America. Includes a character sketch and criticism of his works to date.

———. "Roadside Meetings of a Literary Nomad," *Bookman* (New York), LXXI (June, 1930), 302-13. Characterizes prominent literary figures of the 1890's who were Garland's friends. Information about Zangwill based on Zangwill's 1898 visit to America and Garland's 1899 visit to London.

GOLDING, LOUIS. "The Poet of the Ghetto," *Reconstructionist*, XXIV (Apr. 4, 1958), 28-29. Review of Leftwich's *Israel Zangwill* leads to Golding's personal recollection of Zangwill. Predicts a day when Zangwill's rich talent will again be recognized.

———. "Zangwill the Man," *Fortnightly Review*, CXXI, n.s. (Apr. 1, 1927), 519-28. Characterizes Zangwill as Golding knew him.

GROSS, JOHN. "Zangwill in Retrospect," *Commentary*, XXXVIII (Dec., 1964), 54-57. Review of Wohlgelernter's *Israel Zangwill: A Study*. Finds Zangwill historically significant but of little artistic worth.

HARRIS, ISIDORE. "Mr. Israel Zangwill Interviewed," *Bookman* (London), XIII (Feb., 1898), 145-58. (Also in *Bookman* [New York], VII [Apr., 1898], 104-7.) Traces Zangwill's career; describes his home, his interests, and his method of work. Quotes Zangwill on art. Some critical commentary.

HINDUS, MILTON. "Bard of the Melting Pot," *New Leader*, XLI (Feb. 3, 1958), 25-26. Review of Leftwich's *Israel Zangwill*. Sees Zangwill as "divided, contradictory, torn" on almost every subject, but giving brilliant expression to his ambivalence.

JACKSON, HOLBROOK. "Israel Zangwill," *Bookman* (London), XLVI (May, 1914), 67-73. (Also in *Living Age*, CCLXXXII [Sept. 26,

1914], 790-97.) Reviews Zangwill's work to date, with perceptive analysis of his presentation of the "eternal tragedy of Israel in the light of modern experience."

KORG, JACOB. Rev. of Leftwich, *Israel Zangwill, Victorian Studies,* I (June, 1958), 378-79. Appreciative estimate of Zangwill as artist, placing him in the tradition of English, not Jewish, literature.

LANDA, M. J. "Israel Zangwill, The Dreamer Awake," *Contemporary Review,* CXXX (Aug., 1926), 316-20. Obituary of Zangwill. Especially appreciative of *Children of the Ghetto.* Much on Zangwill's attempt to gain recognition as a dramatist and his attitude toward Zionism (with which Landa disagreed).

LEFTWICH, JOSEPH. "Israel Zangwill," *Transactions of the Jewish Historical Society of England,* XVIII (1953-55), 77-88. A Memorial Lecture delivered before the Jewish Historical Society of England on Mar. 3, 1952. Anecdotal; informative; highly appreciative of Zangwill's work.

―――. "Israel Zangwill: On the Threshold of His Centenary," *Jewish Book Annual,* XXI (1963–64), 104-16. Defends Zangwill's timelessness; asks for a reexamination of his best works and a reassessment of him.

MANKOWITZ, WOLF. "Israel Zangwill," *Spectator,* CXCIII (Aug. 13, 1954), 205. Review of Rodale Press edition of *The King of Schnorrers.* Finds Zangwill typical of working-class artists, who believe that evil is curable by education. Criticizes Zangwill's failure to recognize man's irrationality.

MOULT, THOMAS. "Israel Zangwill," *Bookman* (London), LXX (Sept., 1926), 288-90. Obituary of Zangwill by a personal friend. Contains brief appreciative account of Zangwill's best work.

PARROTT, T. M. "Israel Zangwill—Playwright," *Booklovers Magazine* (later *Appleton's*) (New York), IV (Aug., 1904), 233-38. Begins with a sympathetic review of the successful New York production of *Merely Mary Ann.* Evaluates all of Zangwill's work to date and finds it lacking; sees drama as Zangwill's best hope for future development as artist. Wrong-headed but interesting.

PETERSON, ANNAMARIE. "Israel Zangwill (1864–1926): A Selected Bibliography," *Bulletin of Bibliography and Magazine Notes,* XXIII (Sept.–Dec., 1961), 136-40. Lists Zangwill's "books and plays published in English . . . and as many of the pamphlets as could be traced," "published writings . . . NOT included in his published books," and references to unpublished plays.

SCHWEID, MARK. "Israel Zangwill (On the 25th Anniversary of his Death)," *Jewish Book Annual,* IX (1950), 107-13. Traces Zangwill's life and work, with emphasis on Zangwill's contributions to Jewish culture. Calls *Dreamers of the Ghetto* Zangwill's masterpiece. Finds Zangwill still one of the brightest lights in modern Jewish life. (In Yiddish)

SMERTENKO, JOHAN J. "Israel Zangwill," *Nation* (New York), CXVII (Oct. 31, 1923), 483-84. Defends Zangwill's artistry over "the piddling of Pinero, the baroque of Barrie, and the raucous novels . . . of our youngest generation."

WOLF, LUCIEN. "Literature Portraits—XXXII. Mr. Israel Zangwill," *Literature* (London), IX (Dec. 14, 1901), 549-50. Analyzes Zangwill as characteristic of Jewish genius. Offers sound criticism of the ghetto works, especially *Children of the Ghetto,* and recounts Wolf's role in getting Zangwill a commission to write it.

# *Index*

(The works of Zangwill are listed under his name.)

Maeterlinck, Maurice, 28
Malamud, Bernard, 145-46
Mazzini, Giuseppe, 117, 119
Mendelssohn, Moses, 151
Moses, 32, 138

Oliphant, James, 19

Pain, Barry, 26
*Pall Mall Magazine, The*, 25-26
Pater, Walter, 28

Roosevelt, Theodore, 110
Rossetti, Dante Gabriel, 74
Roth, Philip, 145-46

Schilling, Bernard N., 63
Shakespeare, William, 49, 91
Shaw, Bernard, 20, 120-21, 132
*Society*, 39
Spinoza, Baruch, 150-51
Stevenson, Robert Louis, 28
Swinburne, Algernon Charles, 49, 117, 119

Tolstoy, Leo, 114
Tree, Sir Herbert Beerbohm, 114, 143
Turgenev, Ivan, 27
Twain, Mark, 45-46, 84

Verlaine, Paul, 28

Walkley, A. B., 110
Wallant, Edward, 145-47
Ward, Mrs. Humphrey, 27, 52, 61-63, 84
Webb, Sidney, 36
Wilde, Oscar, 27, 28, 50
Wohlgelernter, Maurice, 23, 24, 63, 67, 117
Wolf, Lucien, 25
World War I, 23, 24, 32, 33, 36, 37, 124

Zangwill, Edith Ayrton, 23
Zangwill, Israel: birth, 20; childhood, 20; at Jews' Free School

as student, student-teacher, 20, 21; work in Zionist movement, 23-24; break with it, 23; work in Jewish Territorial Organization (ITO), 23-24

WORKS:

"Abolition of Money, The," 28
"Adon Olam," 139
"Alla Cantatrice," 137
"Anglicization," 92, 96, 105
"Apres," 135-36
"Art in England," 28
"Asti Spumanti," 138
"At the Dawn," 140-41
"At the Worst," 134, 136
"At the Zoo," 135
"Atonement Hymn," 139
"Authors and Publishers," 28
"Awkward Age of the Women's Movement, The," 34-35
*Bachelor's Club, The,* 21, 39, 46-52, 103
"Bearer of Burdens, The," 91-92, 105
"Bethulah," 99
*Big Bow Mystery, The,* 100
*Blind Children,* 133-39
"Blind Children," 134-35
"Bohemia and Verlaine," 28
"Bridge, The," 136
"Budapest," 28
"Carpenter's Wife, The," 29-30
*Celibates Club, The,* 21, 46-51
"Chad Gadya," 147-49, 153
"Chassé-Croisé," 104
"Chastity," 137
"Cheating the Gallows," 101
"Child of the Ghetto, A," 147-49
*Children of the Ghetto,* 21, 25, 35, 39, 52-63, 83-84, 86, 87, 92, 106, 107 (unpublished play), 145, 146, 148, 149
*Chosen Peoples,* 26
*Cockpit, The,* 126-30, 132
"Concerning General Elections," 28
"Conciliator of Christendom," 152